Julian curled his fingers around the loose fabric of my corduroy skirt and pressed his cheek into my leg hard enough to leave imprints from the corduroy on his face. I stroked his hair and reached down to feel his soft curls. The steady pressure of his silence was palpable like a physical pain. I was afraid that if I held him, he could not tolerate the closeness and would squirm away.

I wanted only to uncover his truth and free him from an unreasonable exile, but I knew how high the stakes ran. A child so sensitive could die on the outside, like a domesticated animal set loose, all at once, in the wild.

this child of mine

this child of mine

A THERAPIST'S JOURNEY

MARTHA WAKENSHAW

HARBINGER PRESS

Harbinger Press
2711 Buford Rd. #383
Richmond, VA 23235-2423
840-560-1195
Fax: 840-327-0061
info@harbpress.com

Quote on page xv by Carolyn Forche from
The Angel of History, published by Harpercollins, 1994.

"A Ritual to Read Together" copyright 1960, 1998 by the Estate of William
Stafford. Reprinted from *The Way It Is: New & Selected Poems* with the
permission of Graywolf Press, Saint Paul, Minnesota.

Editing and Book Design: Janice Phelps
Proofreading: Sonja Beal

Publisher's Cataloging-in-Publication
(Provided by Quality Books, Inc.)

Wakenshaw, Martha.
This child of mine : a therapist's journey / by
Martha Wakenshaw. -- 1st ed.
p.cm.
LCCN: 00-102535
ISBN: 0-9674736-0-8

1. Child psychotherapy--Case studies. 2. Children--
Counseling of--Case studies. I. Title.

RJ504W35 2001   618.92'8914
                       QBI00-705

— *To Theresa* —

*for holding the children
with beauty and grace,
and for holding me.*

Table of Contents

PART III:
THE ROAD BACK

PART IV:
BUILDING UP

PART V:
FIERCE WITH REALITY

Acknowledgments

To write is to bear witness to the truth.

I wish to thank several people who have helped me remain true. These are my husband, Tim, guardian of the most pure and honest soul. My children, Molly Rose and Charlie, sprites of energy and joy. (Thanks you guys for all of your "I love you Mom" notes!) My stepson Patrick — we've traveled a long way together. Thanks for your acceptance and for making me laugh. Remember your creative spirit.

My parents for their love, understanding, and growth.

I thank Sharon, poet, writer, and mentor for believing in me and believing in me again.

Jan, healer and woman of unerring love. Gina for sticking with me all the way.

Keith and Janice, my literary parents to whom I owe the life of this book.

And finally, to the children and families who have taught me how to love more deeply, especially Ellie, the keeper of the dollhouse, the keeper of the heart.

Disclaimer

This book contains references to cases that the author has encountered over the years. However, every effort has been made to change all identifying characteristics — including names, descriptions, gender, and other particulars — in order to protect the privacy of those involved. For that reason, any resemblance between persons depicted in the book and real persons are strictly coincidental.

Preface

I began writing *This Child of Mine* when my son was two and my daughter was four years old. At the time, I was juggling the challenges of a working mother. I held a part-time job as an elementary school counselor, but I soon came to realize that in my role both as mother and counselor I was parenting all of the time.

The schoolchildren who came to my office needed to talk and be heard, to feel safe and be able to accept soothing, to learn the simple, but so often unspoken message — that they were valued for just being.

I delighted in the uniqueness of each child, from the kindergartner who played out domestic violence scenes in my sandtray to the sixth-grade girl who was so inhibited with words, but drew watercolor pictures that communicated to me what was in her heart and soul.

As with my own children, my hope was that the children I worked with at Brookwood Elementary would learn to love themselves and develop their own context for safety and growth. That they would learn how to soothe themselves in stressful times (one of the basic psychological skills necessary to healthy human development) and "shoot forth brightly colored blossoms," a phrase I use to describe Julian in the chapter that bears his name.

In the course of my work as a child and family therapist over the last fifteen years, I have worked with hundreds of children and families. I have seen many children with histories of abuse and neglect who have managed to pull through and some who have not.

When I became a mother at thirty-one, I was ill-prepared for the hard work required of the job, despite my intensive work with children of all ages. I struggled with sleep deprivation, bouts of irritability, and innumerable frustrations, but always a love as deep and complete as any I have ever known sustained me.

Motherhood sprung open a heightened awareness of what it meant to be a parent. I saw almost all parents as doing the best they could. I knew that we all made mistakes and could do better. I came to understand the term, "good enough parenting," coined by Dr. Bruno Bettelheim.

I knew that some parents mistreated their children and that usually they had been mistreated by their caretakers. I struggled with wanting to blame them and having compassion for their circumstance that led to their behavior. I was often horrified by the amount of damage that psychological trauma could cause.

I have specialized in treating childhood trauma and in so doing have taken on an awesome task — the task of opening to these children and not taking on their pain to the extent that it disables me. I have not always been successful. In working with my young clients, I have entered into their worlds so deeply that at times I have feared for my own sanity. I have had to face my own obstacles to growth, both as mother and therapist. I have, literally, been brought to my knees in the face of unimaginable suffering and miraculous resiliency.

Before working in the public school system, I worked in therapeutic children's centers, mental health agencies, and as a home-based worker for Head Start. Currently I maintain a private practice in Seattle.

This Child of Mine is as much about my process of becoming a child therapist as it is about my clients. As a parent I have learned to be a better therapist and the reverse is also true — I have learned to be a better parent through my relations with my clients.

This Child of Mine is also about the displaced child in all of us. It is a story of healing; a journey that has no ending, but forever is held by hope.

*"There are times when the child seems delicate,
as if he had not yet crossed into the world."*
—Carolyn Forche

PART I

THOSE WHO CAN'T
FIGHT BACK

*"The best index to a person's character is how he treats people
who can't do him any good,
and how he treats people who can't fight back."*
—Abigail Van Buren

Beginnings

I HAVE LOST INTEREST IN WHAT THE STATE OF WASHINGTON HAS told me, how the evaluating psychologists have warned me, and how the forensic experts think they know everything.

The State Courtesy Supervision Worker (who has never actually met the family), the treating physician, the caseworker, the child's attorney, the mother's attorney, and all of the substitute workers who step in when the assigned workers are called away to more emergent cases are all part of a "team" that is instructed to act in the best interest of the child.

The history, the long and tangled history, of this five year old's life is of vast importance and really of no importance at all when I sit across the table from him listening to his breath go in and out, smelling its sweetness and watching the paper tear as Bailey applies more and more blue watercolor to paper with a twenty-five cent paintbrush from K-Mart.

If you knew a fetus swam in alcohol and cocaine, if you knew this fetus who became an infant was taken care of by a young mother, a teenager actually, ill-prepared for coping with her own life, who swam, herself, in a fog of misunderstanding. If you saw this child wanting and the mother wanting. If you knew the mother loved the child and even so, left him with his birth father, a registered sex offender, and his birth father tired of the child, then three years old, and left him at the County Child Welfare Office's after-hours emergency drop-off. If you knew that the boy and his younger sister were left with a stranger, and the boy and the girl got separated and placed in different foster homes (also ill-prepared, these homes, for life and living)...

Knowing now that all of this is true: that Bailey was physically and in other ways disabused of his humanity and labeled oppositional-defiant and aggressive; that he was punished for wetting the bed; that he became encopretic, that is he pooped in his pants a lot instead of using the toilet; that he swore he saw blood on the floor when there was none; that he was moved to three different homes in three weeks; that when finally his grandmother came from Washington and rescued him and his sister, the State had by then completed a psychiatric evaluation on Bailey and found him to be severely emotionally disturbed. (Hell, he was drawing with crayons on the wall of the examining room.) If you knew this as I know it, would you still wonder about the rest of Bailey? What really happened?

Bailey's history speaks loudly, but his soul speaks louder still. A child cannot be so easily beaten down to where he will not rise again. Bailey has been shaped by the events in his life. He has been viewed as an object rather than a child. The system has taken hold of him, flung him this way and that, assigned him a case number. To many, Bailey is a number. But, no matter how hard the child welfare system wants Bailey to equal the sum total of his history, it's not going to work, because he is a child of mine — a child of ours.

Bailey exhibits sure signs of what we call mental illness. He sees things in the treatment room that I cannot see. He stirs miniature zoo animals in a bath of blue paint and says, "The animals are dirty. They can never get clean. Their mother will be mad." With one hand he stirs, with the other hand he repeatedly grabs handfuls of his T-shirt as if gathering strength for the work of his play.

Bailey is representative of what can happen to a child, and what often does happen to a child, when they are abandoned, neglected, abused.

Bailey

AILEY CAME TO ME FOR PLAY THERAPY IN THE SPRING. I TRIED to separate the boy from his history. I watched Bailey paint and paint, always in blue watercolor, for weeks. Paint until the paper could hold no more and tore in places.

More than watching Bailey paint, it was hearing Bailey paint. I sat across from him at the play table and listened to his breathing become slow and steady and deep. Bailey went into his work, and I went with him. We traveled together and when we came out, the world looked strange and new. The world looked stark, full of plain objects — matter without soul. Inside the painting is where we both lived.

While we played, Bailey watched out for the "bad guy." Bailey wasn't clear who the bad guy was or how many of them there were. Bailey looked up from his painting now and then to make sure the bad guy wasn't crouched in the corner of my office or hiding underneath my desk. During the first six weeks of treatment, Bailey opened every file drawer, desk drawer, and cabinet to make sure that the bad guy wasn't hiding there. He looked behind the couch and sometimes worked on his painting with a red, plastic bat by his side.

After a couple of months, painting gave way to working with Playdough. Bailey's play became thematic; children trapped in the clay, the bad guy able to transform himself and appear on the couch, in the clock, in the stapler, or get lost in a box of zoo animals.

Bailey worked the blue Playdough and said, "The kids are lost in here. Get them out. They're lost. He used the knife to chop the imaginary children out. "Both are out ... there goes one in again!" Then the Playdough turned into a snake. (Snakes became a recurring theme in Bailey's play.) "They're stuck in the snake. I'm getting them out. (He saws the Playdough snake with knife). "Kids come out , come out. The kids are afraid — Oh no! The kids are inside. They got out. They're free. They're laughing. Stop it you snake!"

During the dialogue with the snake and the kids and himself, Bailey would take breaks to look at me. He left the playroom twice to make sure his grandmother was still waiting for him in the waiting room.

I liked seeing movement in Bailey's play — his ability to make up stories — although I wasn't sure he was able to differentiate from what was happening on the table and what was going on in himself. Bailey often talked about his heart being in his stomach or of dreams where he was reduced to bones with no heart. There seemed to be no container for this child's soul.

Bailey remained full of the many bad guys or monsters that lived inside his head. He continued to have nightmares and to dissociate (mentally leave his body) when stressors in his life or memories became too overwhelming for him to integrate into his four-year-old psyche.

When I sat with Bailey, I felt reduced to my own essence, to the steel girders of my soul. Bailey spoke truth in every word and action. I found myself searching for the truth in everything I did and said. With Bailey, there was nothing contrived. It was all primary process or pure emotive power. His raw energy was contagious and rushed through me like a storm-risen river sweeping away all the detritus. I was left with my whole and imperfect self. At times, the pieces of my own self disengaged — floating in space waiting for some other force to bring them all together again. In helping Bailey remake himself I had to remake myself.

"The boy got hit 'cause he wasn't listening." Bailey says this as he plants two different rubber stamp shapes on the paper and says: "This is you and this is me." I am the multi-pointed star shape. Bailey is the stamp that has a tiny bee on it and says, "Good job!" Bailey is almost five and cannot draw representational figures of people. Even stick figures require too much organized thinking. It's like the gears have disengaged, and he's left with the engine running in neutral. The closest Bailey gets to a human form is a swirl of blue scribble which may start as Bailey or his grandmother or me and then turn into a "hand monster," or a "snake."

Bailey will often pick up another marker in his left hand and have the two colors fight each other. It is usually black that overcomes and blots out blue. Often, the scribbles become so fierce that Bailey is convinced they are spiraling off the page, ready to attack. I suggest taking the paper and tearing it into little pieces, crushing the fragments, and throwing them away in the garbage can of another office. Bailey says, "They can still get out." I motion to the stapler and Bailey folds the paper and staples furiously but cannot get enough staples in fast enough to contain the monster. The monsters start leaking out and getting into everything — the clock, the miniature kangaroo, the dollhouse, the toy box, the inside of my pen. I take the magic wands down and hand Bailey his blue one with the liquid stars and moons inside. Bailey sighs. He starts up with his usual invocation: "Magic wand, magic wand, make the monsters disappear." We wave our wands over the couch, the desk, the clock, the toy box, my pen, everywhere the monster has been.

Bailey suddenly collapses onto the floor and says, "The boy is dying." I pull out the doctor's kit and rush to the scene before me on the carpet. I grip a fleece blanket and throw it over Bailey. I tuck the edges in close around him. I take his pulse and listen through his back for his heartbeat. I tell him that I can feel his heart beating. Bailey says, "Yes, but the boy's arm is broken." (Bailey would refer to himself in our play sessions as "the boy," when he felt overwhelmed and was in pieces — many small Baileys speaking in different voices). I wanted to help Bailey get a sense of his body back. The "broken arm" presented itself as an opportunity.

I palpitate the flesh all along Bailey's forearm. Then I touch his wrist bones. Bailey is small for his age. I find the bones along his hand and delineate each knuckle on each of his fingers. His fingers wiggle in response to my touch. It is not often that Bailey lets me touch him. When he wants a hug or I ask him if it's okay for me to hug him, Bailey lowers his eyes, comes slowly toward me and turns around so that I hug him from behind.

I point out Bailey's veins and bones to him. He is curious as if he has never seen them before. He appears surprised that his physical body belongs to him. The tracing of my fingers over his arm puts a physical boundary around Bailey that helps contain the turmoil that rages inside of him. With a greater sense of his body and his body connected to the earth, Bailey can have a starting place from which to heal.

In this particular play therapy session, Bailey replays the "boy is dying," scenario eleven times. After I check his broken arm, I apply a small plastic cast to it. Bailey lets me rub his back through the blanket.

When Bailey is done with the work of being broken and healed, broken and healed, he springs up and stands on a chair near the floor lamp. Bailey begins to play with the dimmer switch on the light. It is night and with the lights down in my office, the room darkens into shadows and then goes black. As soon as Bailey turns the light off, he switches it back on. He takes delight in controlling the light switch and the atmosphere of the room. He is at the control switch of his own fears.

Each time that Bailey dims the lights, he says, "Stay where you are, Martha."

I am sitting on the floor about a foot and a half away from Bailey and remain in that spot, following his instructions. Suddenly the room goes black. Bailey leaves the light off for several seconds. I wait for the light to come on again and then I feel a hand on my shoulder, then another hand on my other shoulder. Two hands traveling down my arms and smoothing over the backs of my hands. I feel a child's fingers explore my face and touch my hair and feel my earrings. My eyes blink as the light suddenly switches back on to maximum brightness.

Session Notes

Sept. 15: My office is about 8 x 10. It is small enough to be cozy and not so small that it is claustrophobic. Bailey is wearing a red Rugrats T-shirt and jeans. His hair is dark and cut neat. His eyes are almost always wide open. He laughs more than he smiles and that is not much. He laughs when he can engage me in a game of chase. He plays other games like telling me to sit in a chair and not move and then turns all the lights off in the office one by one. It's nightime so the office gets pretty dark except for the glow of the streetlights that leak in through the windows.

My office is near the fire and police departments so sirens often wail during our sessions. When this happens, Bailey crawls under the table and says, "The police are coming for me." When children are placed into protective custody, it is usually by a police car or state- or county-designated vehicle.

Nov 10: Bailey fills a jug with water and carries it to the play table. He has not been interested in painting for weeks. He has reduced his play to plain water which he spills onto the table from paper coffee cups and then wipes up with paper towels. It's a controlled spill, but even so, the water at times almost reaches the radio and then I intervene with some mop up of my own. When this happens, Bailey says, "That must have been scary for you when the water got too close."

Last night, we used an entire roll of paper towels with Bailey tipping the cups, holding out his hand for a towel, me ripping one off the roll, and him wiping. We did not talk — for forty-five minutes — during this ritual except for his comment about me being scared about the radio getting wet. Bailey made sure to get every drop. He put his face almost on the table, scrubbing off whatever he saw there.

But mostly I think he spilled the water a hundred times, wondering if he would be admonished.

Bailey replays the light game three more times, each time reading me like a blind person might. When he is done, he turns on the light and sits on my lap, pressing his back into my chest. I wrap my arms around him and rest my head on his head. It is the first time in six months of therapy that Bailey has allowed me to hold him.

— 📖 —

I flip through Bailey's drawings. They are all slight variations of scribbled pages bound in an orange cover that says, "Bailey's October Journal." It is something he has done with his kindergarten class. I stop on the page that is labeled in a teacher's hand, "Sunny and dark!" I wonder what the exclamation mark is for. The picture speaks for itself. Yellow on blue scribbled out in black.

I'm sitting in a cafe looking at this child's drawings. There is an elderly couple at the next table drinking cappuccino and talking art with the proprietor. The woman has a British accent. The man is wearing a large knit fisherman's sweater with a silver cross around his neck. His partner peruses an art magazine. They are talking about DaVinci, the Louvre, how much sleep they got last night. Their conversation appears trivial next to the power of Bailey's drawings.

Tomorrow I will meet with Bailey's grandmother. Her face is careworn and beautiful. She has told me that she can do this — raise Bailey and his sister, Carrie, as long as she can see the light at the end of the tunnel. The light is her daughter getting custody of the kids back. I want to hold that light for her, but I know that that would be a lie. This story may not have a happy ending.

What are Bailey's drawings trying to tell me? Blue on blue on blue again. Black on blue on yellow. Someone has helped him name this one — "Big Color Monster!"

The page that I'm most interested in has no caption. There are four distinct scribbles in blue marker, the middle one scribbled over so many times that the paper is torn. It's the biggest of four scribble blobs. The blobs are cocoon-like in the way the pen lines have wrapped themselves around and around each other. Above the blobs float three squiggly lines — hieroglyphics of some sort and above these, four random lines, all in blue. Untitled. Do the blobs represent people? Possibly. The next page is also untitled: a much looser scribble with a dark blob off to one side. The picture after that is virtually the same only it is named in an adult's handwriting: "This is a man that turned into a snake. A very big, big snake. It has clothes on!"

— 📖 —

It's been about a year that I've been seeing Bailey. I was on vacation for ten days so I missed our appointment one week, but sent him a postcard from Florida with a pink flamingo on it. He remembered the bird when I got back. He remembered the flamingo first, and then he remembered me and circled the waiting room walking around the carpet on his tiptoes saying, "I- I- I was going to make you a card. It was going to say 'I love you.'"

There is talk of sending Bailey to a home in southern Oregon for attachment disordered kids.

— 📖 —

I am aware that in my own early life there has been trauma. Bailey is new to me, yet so familiar. It is like I have known him for a very long time. I feel myself going with him more and more. Leaving my body and entering into some other world that speaks only emotion. When the emotions get too strong I feel myself longing to disappear and it is frightening this feeling of being pulled into the unknown.

With Bailey, I remain professionally responsible. I am able to pull myself back down to earth when I start going too deep, because he needs me here when he returns — the welcoming mother.

In my own therapy sessions, when I sit with Jan, the pull becomes stronger and stronger until it takes over, and I am gone for increasingly longer periods. It starts with feeling so vulnerable that I believe she can see right through me. The feeling is acutely uncomfortable and seeks release somewhere. I become hypervigilant. I look around her office for places to hide. Finding none I withdraw into myself. Like a child, I believe that if I close my eyes she cannot see me. Next, my body. I become disembodied and a sense of numbness pervades my being. I hear Jan's voice receding as I recede and it becomes easier to disappear. My strongest desire is to become invisible and yet it is also the scariest place to go — feeling so disconnected from the earth, from what holds me here. The clinical name for these symptoms is Post-traumatic Stress Disorder. It occurs when a person is repeatedly exposed to envinronmental stress that is too overwhelming for them to integrate.

Billie

I LISTEN TO THE COOKS SPEAKING VIETNAMESE. THEIR VOICES sound like a sweet song. The gray November sky surrounds my ground-floor, corner office. The trees stripped of their autumn color stand in carefully placed intervals along the sidewalk.

Steel-cut oats bubble in fat, round pots and fill the hallways and classrooms with a heavenly scent. The galley-style kitchen is small for an institutional setting. The cooks are paid minimum wage to boil hot dogs and heat macaroni and cheese out of a can. On holidays they make spring rolls and bring them to me on a child's plastic saucer.

I pull my blue cardigan close around me. The heating system has been on the blink. Although we cannot afford it, I have called the repair service. The money will have to come from somewhere. Some of the children have been getting sick.

The vans arrive at the therapeutic child care center. I watch the stream of children flow up the sidewalk; some of the staff hold babies in their arms, and children up to age five unload in pairs, holding hands.

I am two months into my first job as a case manager at a non-profit agency that serves abused and neglected preschoolers. I am twenty-seven years old and single. I have the eagerness and courage of a newcomer and a fair amount of idealism which I prefer to think of as hope.

The children exhale rings of frost into the chilly morning air. They are bundled in bulky coats with hoods or heavy wool sweaters with the cuffs rolled up. Every year we have a clothing drive and the donations carry the kids through all the seasons.

At the end of the line I see Billie, a tall and skinny two year old, moving up the sidewalk holding the hand of his teacher. Billie is on my caseload, one of twenty three children that were referred to Kid's Place by Child Protective Services (CPS). Billie's mom is African-American, his dad is Caucasian, and Billie has beautiful mocha-colored skin and an irresistible grin that is rarely seen.

Today, Billie stands out from the other children because he isn't wearing a coat or pants or a shirt or shoes. He is wearing a pillowcase for a diaper. All that he has on is this yellowed rectangle of thin cotton pulled between his legs and fastened on one side with a safety pin. The other side is knotted at the toddler's waist. Billie looks like a miniature Christ figure, bare-foot, bare-chested, a winding mass of cloth swathed around his emaciated torso. (I don't know that I will see Billie again in ten years, a moustache on his upper lip, his arms encircling a basketball.)

The image of Billie stays in my mind throughout the day. I will have to call his mother and his CPS caseworker, too. The pillow-case most likely means that his mother is using again: trading her food stamps or her body for drugs. I will send some diapers home with Billie on the van — try and scrounge a coat and some clothing from the donations in the basement. This could mean a return to foster care for Billie. He has already been in and out of three foster placements since his birth. The moves are devastating to a child this age. The pain of separating from his mother unimaginable. Despite her habit she dearly loves her only son. Severing the attachment to his mother each time Billie is sent to foster care is like cutting away at a steel cable with a pair of scis-sors. I learn quickly that most of the abused and neglected kids I work with love their parents best.

If Billie's CPS worker decides to take action on grounds of neglect she will notify his mother and say this: "Your child has been placed in protective custody. In seventy-two hours there will be a shelter-care hearing and you must be present if you have any concern at all for your child's welfare."

A shelter-care hearing means a visit to juvenile court where a judge decides, after hearing the evidence, how long the child should remain in protective custody. Sometimes the child is returned directly after the hearing. Sometimes the child remains in foster care with a hearing scheduled three months down the road. During this time, the parent is required to do certain things to get their child back: attend a series of parenting classes, go for drug/alcohol treatment or anger management classes. The prescription is different for each family depending on the circumstances.

Billie's mother, Lorraine, has failed substance abuse treatment three times and is back on the street trying to make a living as a prostitute. Lorraine isn't sure who Billie's father is so she doesn't waste time telling Billie about a dad.

Marty

I T IS PART OF MY MORNING RITUAL TO WATCH THE CHILDREN arrive. My office has big floor-to-ceiling windows. I often help the children off the bright blue vans. I especially like the feeling of a bundled baby in my arms.

After the children arrive I go to all the classrooms to greet them and take attendance. Only three out of fifty-five kids are absent. I write their names on my clipboard, and before calling their homes I stop in the kitchen to prepare another cup of coffee. The kitchen is the center of Kid's Place. The Vietnamese cooks who work there are always ready with a smile and a few kind words. They take great care with every dish they make whether it is tomato soup out of the can or homemade macaroni and cheese, the kids' favorite. Everyday at three o'clock when it is snack time for the kids, Ming brings me a plate of fruit and cheese or an oatmeal cookie and some juice in a plastic glass.

Today I talk with the cooks for awhile. They are busy rolling out dough for homemade biscuits. We talk about Thanksgiving and the holiday season. They promise a meal of spring rolls and "Vietnamese food — good!" for the day before Christmas Eve. The kitchen feels warm and safe. I don't want to leave it.

I return to my office and sip my coffee. There are two columns of newspaper lain out on my desk. The headline is in small bold print and reads, "Body Found in Motel Room." The article suggests that a woman has overdosed on drugs and died in a back room of the Windmill Motel. She was found at about five o'clock in the morning when the manger went on a routine check of the building.

16

The body is identified as that of Mariah Winchell. Mariah's son Marty, age four, attends our school. His mother died last night. Was he there? Did he see? Did he know? Would he come to school today? When I had gone to Mary's classroom to check attendance he was absent. I go back to the room just to make sure. Marty often comes to the center late. He's not there. I figure Marty won't come to school on the day that his mother has died.

In the storeroom I pack some disposable diapers into a paper bag and write "BILLIE" on the bag in huge block letters with a black magic marker. I go to Billie's classroom and put the bag in his cubby. He is seated at the breakfast table eating a steaming bowl of oatmeal, in a blue V-neck sweater that hangs just below his knees.

At lunchtime, Marty shows up holding the hand of his deceased mother's boyfriend. Marty calls his mom's boyfriend, "Uncle Eddie." All the staff at Kid's Place know Uncle Eddie. He liked to surprise Marty with a trip downtown for new shoes or a picnic in the park. Marty would tell me how Uncle Eddie liked to twirl him up in the air and let him ride on his shoulders on the way to the park.

I send Marty to his classroom so Eddie and I can talk. Marty looks the same: rumpled button-down shirt and baggy jeans, his blond hair sticking out in cowlicks and a slightly unfocused look in his eyes that makes him appear goofy. I expect him to look different because of what has happened.

Eddie sits down in the threadbare armchair opposite mine and says, "I'm sorry Ma'am." I say that I am sorry too, sorry about the death of the boy's mother, sorry that Eddie has lost half of what he lived for, sorry for all the bad luck in the world.

Hunched over in the armchair, his head in his hands, Eddie asks me if I will write a letter on his behalf, "You know just something that says I'll be a good father to the boy." Marty is one of the lucky ones. There is someone to care for him. A person who cares makes all the difference, all the difference in the world to a child.

Marrisa

I KNEW THAT I HAD TO GET A TOUGHER SKIN IF I WERE TO KEEP working at Kid's Place. So much of the job was fun — playing hide and seek with the kids on the playground, eating lunch with them seated in tiny kid chairs with my knees scrunched up to my chin, rubbing the children's backs while they went down for nap. But there was the awful stuff too: kids showing up with unexplained bruises and burns, kids coming to the center with the same diaper I had sent them home in the night before, three-year-olds playing house and the one playing the dad saying things like, "Get outta my face you mothafucker."

I didn't hate the parents and caretakers of the kids that came to Kid's Place. My friends said, "I could never do what you're doing. I would kill the parents." I didn't like what some of the parents did to their kids, but I saw them mostly as victims of their own upbringing. The generational learning, the doing as only they knew how, the poverty and ugliness ever present in their lives. Some tried to break the chain.

Three-year-old Marissa and her mother, Charlotte, were trying to make a go of providing some kind of life for themselves. Charlotte was sixteen when she got pregnant with Marissa. The father, Tony, tried to stay involved, but he was young, too, and his family kept pulling at him to finish high school and pretend that his baby was never going to come. Marissa came into the world on July 5, two months premature, weighing just under five pounds. At two years old she tested within developmentally appropriate guidelines for her age despite the fact that her mother was considered developmentally delayed with an I.Q. score of seventy-seven.

Despite Marissa's environmental stressors: poverty, isolation, a mother who couldn't decipher the directions on the formula can and fed her daughter sugar and water instead — Marissa thrived. It was when a neighbor complained to CPS that the child was left for long periods of the evening alone while her mother was out doing "God knows what," and that "All kinds of strange men kept coming to the apartment at all hours," that Marissa got referred to us.

On my home visit to enroll Marissa, Charlotte greeted me at the door in a worn terry cloth robe. Her smile revealed several missing teeth. Charlotte offered me a seat and a cup of coffee. I accepted both and, as she lit up a cigarette, I asked where Marissa was.

"Marissa," Charlotte yelled, "get your butt out here. There's a lady want to see you."

Marissa came scampering out to the cluttered living area, her long blond hair in tangles down to her waist. Her face was dirty and her hands were sticky when she reached out to take the box of crayons and pad of drawing paper I had brought her. Charlotte handed me a cup of coffee and said, "Sorry no cream and sugar if you take it." I took the coffee and watched Marissa play on the carpet that was littered with fast food wrappers, crumbs of food and Playdough. Charlotte cleared a place on the coffee table for me to lay out my enrollment papers and sucked on her cigarette.

Charlotte was candid about her situation. "It ain't easy raising a kid you know — especially by yourself. Do you have any kids?" As usual I felt accused when the parents of the kids I enrolled found out I didn't have any of my own. There was Kitty who showed me the dent in the wall where she had thrown her son's toy rockinghorse in a fit of rage. "Of course, you wouldn't understand that — not having kids of your own."

I talked mostly with Charlotte about what Marissa liked to play with and what kinds of food she liked. I wanted to know how the adjustment to Kid's Place would be for her.

Before I left, Charlotte told me that she was desperate for

food for "the baby," which was how she referred to Marissa and that she wanted to find a job and get off welfare. I gave her some resources in the community for food banks and told her I could help with some referrals for job training. I told her to have Marissa ready for the van to pick her up at eight thirty-five the following Monday.

Marissa was ready on time every day for the first two weeks. I called Charlotte to get her to join the weekly parent group and come in to talk about job training, but I didn't hear a word from her.

The third week that Marissa was at Kid's Place, her CPS caseworker called. I wasn't prepared for the history I was to hear and felt like closing my ears while she talked on and on about the repeated incidence of neglect since birth. The reports from the public health nurse said that Marissa was suffering from malnutrition. The reports from neighbors said that the child slept on a mattress on the floor while her mother had sex with different men she would bring home from the tavern after leaving Marissa home alone for hours.

The thing I remember most about this conversation with the caseworker was that there were "cat hairs stuck in Marissa's dirty diaper." I really didn't see what that had to do with anything, but I did understand that this child was severely neglected. Barb told me that if another report came in she was going to petition the court to remove the child from the home and place her in protective custody.

The thought of Marrisa separated from her mother was unimaginable. The two were closely bonded. I knew that Charlotte was struggling to keep her daughter fed and clothed, but there was no lack of love here. It was like Charlotte needed a mother herself and then she could mother Marissa and learn that leaving a toddler alone for hours was considered to be neglectful and damaging to a young child.

I tried to help Charlotte learn to be a more responsible mother. At first she heeded my advice about not leaving Marissa alone even for a minute and fixing her a good dinner every day, not just on days when she felt like it. (Marissa got breakfast and lunch at school everyday). The more I tried to help Charlotte, the more I felt like I was losing the battle. Charlotte appeared to be incapable of maintaining even a shred of consistency and organization in her life. The public health nurse assigned to the family taught Charlotte about bathing Marissa and cooking simple, nutritious meals, but Charlotte would call me to say she was out of soap or she couldn't remember how to fix spaghetti sauce.

Over the next few weeks Marrisa started to decline. She withdrew from other children at school and came to school in the same clothing everyday. After awhile she started to smell. Her hair was matted and dirty and her four front teeth had turned a rusty brown color and she cried every time she bit into a slice of bread at lunch.

I was the one to catalyze the next report which I knew could mean removal of the child from her home. Marissa's teeth got so bad that she couldn't chew and she stopped eating altogether. Repeated attempts to get Charlotte to take her daughter to a dentist failed. She was either too busy or she had run out of bus tickets. Cost was not a problem since I had lined up a dentist to do the necessary work pro bono.

Finally, I took Marissa to the dentist myself and sat in the waiting room while he numbed her mouth and yanked out four rotten-to-the-roots front teeth. The dentist called the caseworker and filed a report of medical neglect. The child had what he called, "Baby Bottle Syndrome." Marissa was sucking down too many bottles of sugar water and her teeth just couldn't take it anymore. (I still have the brown baby teeth in a capsule that the dentist gave me).

When the caseworker's car appeared in the school's driveway, followed by a police car, my dam of denial burst so completely that the center director put her hand on my shoulder and said, "Why don't you take the rest of the afternoon off?" Somehow I didn't think this would really happen. Somehow, I thought that Charlotte would get her act together and care for her child. I felt that Marissa was being stolen from her mother like a common object.

My hope for Marissa was that she would love her new foster

home. Surely she would flourish. Marissa would live in a clean house with a big backyard. She would have her hair washed in rose water and eat with silverware at a big table with other children. She would not have to witness her mother performing sexual acts with strangers in the bedroom that she and Marissa shared. She would sleep in freshly washed sheets in a bed of her own, and she would never come to school hungry and tired and scared.

The air in the crowded office became static after the child was physically taken to live among strangers. I gathered up my coat and briefcase and left. I stepped out into a snowy December afternoon and saw where the tire tracks of the police car had been.

I thought of the foster children, Regina and her brother Joseph, who came to our house after church when I was a girl of eight. I had been mystified with thoughts of what it must be like to live in an orphanage. Regina came from a place called "Hillcrest." I imagined great rolling green hills with a stone mansion set on a rise with blankets of green grass unfolding in all directions. I had romanticized this vision of children living without parents; sleeping in long rows of beds like Madeline. But in my real, grown-up life, the images that came to mind of foster care were not of cozy beds in a row and children having pillow fights, but of tears and sorrow and the depthless pain of separating from a beloved parent.

When I had played with Regina all those Sunday afternoons as a child, I imagined her as my sister. I wanted to live with her in the big, stone mansion that I thought was her home. Twenty years later I would think I felt the pain of Charlotte and Marissa as they tried to find each other in the vast channels of their hearts. Twenty years later, I would remember Regina and my own life as a child and recognize how different we were.

Regina

A CRUSH OF COTTON FIBERS BRUSHED TO A FINE SMOOTHNESS: *black velvet. I can feel the coolness of the inside lining — not the velvet, but some other cloth, something less luxurious, against my skin. A common cloth is pressed next to my body, flat with youngness. My hips and shoulder blades jut out. The dress sprouts a white starched collar. The cuffs are white and starched, too. Three rows of white stitching climb up the front of the dress in an inverted "W."*

I open the dress one Sunday morning before church. It is not a special occasion. Not a holiday, not a birthday. Only a box for me to open in the morning, for no reason in particular.

I remember the slick whiteness of the box, but not as white as the dress's collar and cuffs. The box was plain and unwrapped. It was made from the soft cardboard you find in a department store. After I took the dress out, the sides of the box caved in a little. I wished that the box had been wrapped in a riot of colored paper, but it was plain. I remember the feel of the tissue paper, dry against my hands, so delicate it could melt. I remember the cloying smell of dark velvet. I remember how the dress was folded up carefully. Someone had spent time folding this dress precisely and exactly so it fit into the box perfectly.

I shake out the stiff folds and hold the dress up to my shoulders. The newness excites me. Everyone is watching. My mother smiles. My father smiles. My brothers are in their rooms getting dressed for church. "Go ahead and try it on," my mom says.

I go to my room and slide out of my pajamas still warm with sleep. I shiver in the cold. I pull on cotton underpants and an undershirt. I yank the dress over my head. It feels tight. I am afraid that I might rip the seams. I hear a little sound under one arm like stitches popping, but I keep tugging and the dress comes on.

I go to the living room and stand on the circle of olive green carpet. I turn my back to my mother so that she can zip up the dress. My father gets the camera. I perch on the edge of the marble coffee table for a picture.

In the picture, my legs are bare and crossed. You can see my shin bones. I am wearing black patent leather shoes and white anklets. I am wondering what Regina will think. I feel ashamed that I have a new dress for no reason and she does not. I will want to give her this dress, but I can't, because it belongs to me.

Regina came to our house in the suburbs of New York when I was eight. She only came a few times after church. She stayed with us for a few hours, filling the normally slow Sunday afternoons with magic.

It was always fall when Regina was over. The big-leaved trees outside our bay window were infused with fiery color. When we raked the leaves, I felt alive. My cheeks burnished with the flush of the first frost. We raked great mountains of leaves until the place between my thumb and first finger blistered. Then we let the rake drop and we ran as fast as we could, leaping into the leaves where I would roll and cover myself and smell the freshness of death, of the leaves dying, and the leaves that had died.

Afterward, we would sit on the upholstered couch in the living room and look out on the explosion of fall color. Regina wore a white, cotton dress, a size too small for her that showed off the brownness of her skin. Her arms were bare and I would roll up the sleeves of my Sunday best so that my skin could touch hers. We didn't talk very much. I loved to look down and see our skin in brown and white, our forearms matched in size, touching, as if by accident. We would stay like this and talk a little about what we might do after lunch.

I was careful with Regina. She was like a treasure I had found and I wasn't sure how fragile and delicate or how tough and strong she might be. I remember the calm I felt in her presence. She came over me like a soft blanket. Although we were the same age, I imagined that Regina was my older sister.

I was in love with Regina: the rich brown of her skin so smooth, her head textured into tight knots that quilted her scalp, her fingers so delicate and so long with white crescents at the tip of her fingernails. I recall how bright she was sitting beside me. How straight she sat with her feet not quite touching the floor. I remember the ache of wanting to grab her hand and hold it in mine. I didn't know what she would do, so I settled for my skin against hers, our arms touching, and felt the space between us that got smaller the longer we sat.

I thought Hillcrest, the home for orphaned children, must be a very nice place, because Regina and her brother, Joseph, were such nice kids. Joseph was younger than Regina, and my brothers took him downstairs to the playroom for a game of floor hockey, or outside in the yard to play football.

When I thought of Hillcrest, I imagined this great house set against rolling fields and hardly any adults around so the kids could play all day long and do whatever they wanted and eat whatever they chose and go to bed at all hours of the night. I envied Regina's freedom. At least that's what I thought it was then — freedom. She never talked about what it was like at Hillcrest and I never asked. I liked my fantasies the way they were. Regina's quiet ways were dignified and mysterious. I never once thought that she was sad, but now I do. I think she was sad a lot of times when she came to our house.

Sometimes Regina and I would sit on the couch. I would share my dolls with her, and we wouldn't say much. We would dress and undress the dolls and pretend we were mommies. This is when I wished with my whole heart that Regina was my sister and she could live with us all the time.

During the time that Regina visited I often looked at the clock; for when two o'clock came she would have to go back to Hillcrest. I never got to go with her. My father would drive Regina and Joseph back precisely at two and I would watch through the window, through the maze of colored leaves.

After lunch, Regina and I would go downstairs and sit side by side on the piano bench attempting to play duets. I always played the soprano keys. She played the alto. I don't know if she could read music or not, but the duets always sounded like the singing of angels to me.

When we would go downstairs away from the adults, Regina smiled more. Maybe she was hungry and she felt better after we ate our big Sunday, after-church lunch. Maybe it was getting away from the upstairs — my parent's domain. Whatever the reason, Regina's mouth would stretch large across a row of crooked teeth; her small face would light up with the discovery of a pale pink blossom on the begonia or in hearing the skim ice crackle on our pond outside when her shoes tapped the frosty edges.

The day that I wore my black velvet dress to church was the last day that I saw Regina. She told me that she liked my dress. "That's nice," she said in her deep, smooth-as-glass voice. I looked down and said, "Thanks." I wanted to take the dress off right there, in Fellowship Hall, and give it to her. I knew it would fit. We were about the same size. She was just a little taller and skinnier. I thought that the dress would look beautiful on her, more beautiful than it did on me.

Regina asked me that day on the way home in the car as we sat bunched up together in the back seat of the station wagon if it was my birthday. I said, "No."

Later, a final question: "Can I touch it?"

I said, "Yes," and she brushed her palm down the sleeve of black velvet starting at the shoulder and moving all the way down to the cuff. She stopped at the starched white cuff and did not go any farther. Her rubbing of my sleeve felt like the cascading of cool water.

When we got home that day, the leaves were bright with color and we sat on the couch. I kicked off my black patent leathers, but Regina kept on her regular, everyday shoes.

My mom made us grilled cheese sandwiches and tomato soup. When Regina ate, she bent her head down over her food and didn't come up until she was done. She always said, "Yes, please," to seconds and my mother would fill her bowl and heap her plate. After lunch, we were allowed to take our dessert downstairs.

I didn't change clothes when I got home from church. Regina had nothing to change into so I kept my dress on too, as a sort of pact I had made with myself. More than anything else, I didn't want to be different from her.

The first Sunday without Regina, I came home from church and went to my room. I closed the door and yanked the black velvet over my head. I had to strain to reach the zipper, first grabbing it down from the top and then pulling it the rest of the way from the bottom. My arms ached with the effort. The dress tore an inch or so in the armpit and I wadded it up and threw the ball of cloth to the back of my closet.

I missed Regina as if I had missed the coming of a new season. A bunch of these Sundays went by and Regina still didn't come. Our family went to church, and each week I would look for Regina's knotted hair over the rows of straight and curly and bald heads. I couldn't find her. She didn't come to Sunday school anymore, either, and the teacher said, "Regina will no longer be with us." I thought that Regina must be going to another church and going home with another family.

I remember the time that Regina had laughed when I told her I was playing a sheep in the school play. Her laugh was contagious and soon we both burst open with laughter and rolled together in a tumble onto the floor. I could smell the earth in her skin and the special kind of oil she used in her hair. Her long legs wrapped around mine and we giggled and chased each other on the floor, catching and getting loose, catching and getting loose, black velvet against white cotton.

Director

A FTER A FEW YEARS AT KID'S PLACE, I AM PROMOTED TO director. My skin hasn't gotten any tougher. I start getting headaches and stomachaches and feel physically and emotionally unwell most of the time. I become the director of a Kid's Place center by default; the former director gets pregnant — I wish I could trade places with her. I wish that I were having a baby and she was still in charge.

I'm not used to being in charge and for the first three months in my new position I don't think that I will make it. During this time, I fire a volunteer for wanting to know too much about the kids' personal lives. I have trouble telling her that she's fired. I go around and around the subject talking about the importance of confidentiality and personal privacy, etc. and then she just jumps in with, "You're trying to fire me aren't you?" And I nod my head yes and she gets up and leaves me sitting in my great big swivel chair without another word.

For the nine months I last as director I don't like it much at all. Besides the wear and tear on my body, I feel somehow distanced from the children I have carried in my arms off the vans and colored crayons with on the floor of my office. All of a sudden, I'm a bureaucrat and the children are commodities. Almost my entire job consists of hosting Junior League fundraisers and testifying in court as a professional witness on child welfare hearings.

I have to run staff meetings and hear from employees about what a drag it is to drive the old broken-down vans. One morning I come to work to find twigs and branches stuffed into the gas tanks of all five vans. The vans are inoperable and I want to put my head on my desk and cry. I think that an angry parent must have done this, but then I wonder if a disgruntled staff member did it. The pay is lousy and the work is tough.

One day an exquisite oak rocking chair is donated to the center, and I wish it weren't because immediately the toddler-room teacher and the infant-room teacher are squabbling about who's going to get the chair. In the end I give the chair to the infant room because I've already brought in my own bentwood rocker for the toddler room.

Most times I'm running the center on empty. Funds dry up and so does my energy. I start hearing words like, "co-dependent," and "workaholic," and wonder if that's what I am. I start to wonder about just how far I'll go with this work.

At Christmas time, my third at Kid's Place, I drive through a blizzard to deliver gifts and a meal to one of the families and end up with the van stalled out in a ditch. I leave the van where it is and walk the extra half mile to the family's home. The snowfall makes the neighborhood seem less dangerous than it really is.

I start putting myself into more and more risky situations. When I look back on some of the places I traveled to alone at night to drop off a forgotten child left at the center or to bring a quart of milk up through stairwells filled with drug dealers, I wonder that I'm still alive.

Ray Ray

TO LOOK AT RAYMOND, YOU WOULDN'T KNOW THAT HE GOT himself up hours before the school bus came and picked up clothes off of the floor in the dark and dressed himself so he'd be ready on time. You might wonder what a small boy of four was doing standing at the bus stop in the dark of early morning winter. If you drove by at six thirty a.m., he might be outside in a blue wool cap shifting his thirty-eight pounds from one foot to the other to stay warm, but he wouldn't look at you. He knew better than to interact with strangers. That was one of many survival skills that Raymond, also called Ray Ray, knew.

If you observed Ray Ray at circle time, on most days, you would not pick him out of the crowd of other four and five year olds as any different from the rest.

But there was the time that Ray Ray asked to be excused from circle to go to the boys' bathroom. Ray Ray was good at following the rules. He raised his hand, but only when the teacher had finished talking. He asked politely, "May I please go to the bathroom?" After Ray Ray returned, another boy had to go. Elliott was not gone long. He came back to circle and shouted, "Someone peed the whole bathroom." When the teacher went to check, she found urine sprayed on the mirror and the walls and the inside of the door. There was urine puddling in the sink.

Ray Ray could not explain his actions. The teacher sent him to the bathroom with a bucket of warm sudsy water and a large sponge. It took Ray forty-five minutes to clean the bathroom. When he was done, it sparkled.

On the outside everything about Ray Ray is soft and benign. On the inside, this child is a seething sea of undiluted emotion. Even when Ray Ray is murdering the bad guy in play therapy or choking the plastic shark with his bare hands, there is a gentle fluidity to his actions. Nine times out of ten, after he succeeds in killing the bad guy, Ray Ray calls 911 for an emergency vehicle to take the man to the hospital and see if he can be revived. Usually, he can be. Once revived, Ray Ray becomes all nerves again. He collects play weapons and arms himself with at least two guns and one knife. The bad guy doesn't change just because he dies. He comes back to life badder than ever.

Every day that I see Ray Ray come off the van and into Kid's Place, I am happy to see that he is still alive.

The court assigns me to Ray for play therapy. We meet once a week. It's easy to get started because we already know each other from our years together at Kid's Place. Ray Ray has been coming there since he was two.

Guns are a way of life for Ray Ray and I know that I need to get some toy weapons for him to work through his trauma. When his dad isn't serving time, he keeps a revolver loaded in his top dresser drawer. A gunshot once shattered the living room window of Raymond's home. The window is fixed up with a piece of cardboard and some masking tape. Long-legged cracks spring out from the bullet hole and run all the way down the big picture window. With all the rain we've had lately, the cardboard isn't doing much good anymore.

I go to a toy store and buy a red space gun, a black plastic revolver, a gun that can shoot pieces of potato, and two knives; one plastic and one made of rubber. The plastic knife recedes into its sheath when you stab someone with it. The rubber knife is larger and has a big sheath that can attach to your belt. I feel like I am buying contraband. I know that Ray Ray will love these weapons.

He arrives at his counseling sessions smelling sour and hungry.

We eat coffee cake and drink root beer out of the can before beginning our play therapy. He carries the box of toys to the playroom
struggling under their weight. He will not let me help him. I give
him the keys to the playroom and he opens the door.

One of the first things that Raymond does in play therapy is
buy me a gun. He purchases the gun with phony paper money
and hands the black plastic revolver to me. "Here. You take
this. You might need it."

Raymond stuffs another gun inside his pants next to the soft
flesh of his belly and another red space gun goes into his
pocket. On second thought, he takes the space gun out of his
pocket and hands it to me. "You could get run over. Your
boyfriend could bust your door down and beat you." I take the
gun and the instructions that go with it from a four year old.

Raymond circles the playroom feeling safe enough to
explore, once armed with the toy guns he has found. It takes
awhile to get the bad guy and, once gotten, he keeps popping
up again like characters in horror movies that you think are
dead and then scream when they come to life once more.

In our second session of play therapy, Raymond puts on a
pirate's hat and a pair of sunglasses. The sunglasses are too big
for him and slide off his nose. He finds the weapons again and
divides them out between the two of us.

Ray Ray shoots me with the revolver and then cuts off my
head with the large knife. The teddy bear in the corner of the
room gets the same treatment.

Immediately after killing us, Ray takes out the doctor's kit
and bandages me up. Then he takes the teddy bear to a nursing
home and leaves him there with a box of Band-Aids. "That will
make it safe for him to go home," he says gesturing to the bear.

"The bad guy is at the nursing home," Ray tells me. "Quick,
we got to go!"

For twenty minutes we fire at the bad guy, but he won't die.
He keeps popping up like a toy punching bag clown.

Our time is almost up, and the bad guy is still haunting Ray;
springing up from behind bookcases and pouncing at him from
underneath chairs.

I say, "I am the police. Step aside." Then I take out my gun and shoot the bad guy three times. "Dead," I say. "The bad guy is dead."

Ray Ray lets out a long sigh and sits on the floor with his hand still clutching his gun. When I tell him that our time is up for the day, Ray puts away the toys without me having to ask him. As we walk down the hall to join the rest of the class for recess, Ray says, "Got anything to eat?"

—— 📖 ——

It's recess at Kid's Place. I watch Raymond run, ruddy-cheeked, in a Chicago White Sox baseball hat. He is a gray streak against the backdrop of trees that are beginning to turn color with the coming of fall.

Detective Mills has come to interview Raymond on the child abuse incident that landed his dad in jail. The interview at this stage is kind of a technicality. Ray has already talked to the folks at Child Protective Services and told them the truth about his dad slapping him back and forth across the face.

I slip into my coat and walk to the edge of the outdoor play area with the detective. He wants to observe Ray for awhile before talking to him.

"You've got the making of a sociopath there," Detective Mills tells me out on the play field gesturing toward Ray Ray. "Eighty percent of all criminals were abused as children," he says, flicking the ashes of his cigarette into the wind.

BAD BOY

It had been around the first of December when Raymond came to school with bruises on his face. He said he couldn't talk about it. "I'm not supposed to talk about it. I'll get in trouble. I ran into some thorn bushes."

Band-Aids crisscrossed both of his cheeks, the smell rubbery and damp. A handprint hid behind the Band-Aids, but the fingerprints were visibly spoking out from underneath the bandages.

Raymond's eyes stayed wide open and scanned the room as the caseworker from Child Protective Services interviewed him. "I can't talk about it," he repeated.

The child's eyes are dull. His mouth betrays him as it twists and cries. It talks. It tells the man what it has been sworn not to tell.

Bad boy.

His mother, Darlene, calls him "nappy-headed" and grins. She has been clean now for eight months. Her eyes are bright and her face looks new like all the dead and angry layers of skin have been peeled away. She makes it to work on time at the nursing home four out of five days a week.

His father is booked on assault charges against his four-year-old son. Ray's mother tries to tell the policemen that Ray fell against a thorn bush, and that's how his face got all beat up.

Ray watches as his father is stuffed into the patrol car, hands cuffed behind his back.

He thinks...

It is because of me that my mom is crying. It is because of me that my dad is being hauled off to jail again. I shouldn't have been messing around in his dresser drawers. I shouldn't have touched his gun. I shouldn't of stolen the dollar bill.

Bad Boy.

The policeman comes for me. Everyone is talking. "How old are you?" I hold up four fingers, one, two, three, four. I can count to ten. I want a ride in that car. The kids at school won't believe it.

The policeman's face is smooth like beach rocks. He gives me a teddy bear. It is white and fuzzy. Everyone is talking.

I get a lot of things. Crayons and colored paper, juice, and crackers, a toothbrush, underpants in the package. The package crinkles when I touch it.

I get stuffed animals. They are s'posed to stay at school. My teacher says, "Take them."

I start to cry.

My teacher hugs me. I put my head in her chest. I look up, she is not Mama.

My teacher says I am going to a safe place. It is something called a foster home.

I can't stop crying.

***

My dad smells like beer and smoke and pee. His breath stinks. I get myself small like the hamster in the cage at school.

My dad wears a gold ring with a diamond inside.

Thunder comes in my ears and lights come into my eyes.

I can't breathe.

He slaps me back and forth and back and forth.

My face is burning hot. My mother is crying.

Bad boy.

***

I get into the cop car. The siren doesn't go on. I want the policeman to turn on the siren. I am afraid. Not even one time ... he doesn't turn the siren on.

I close my eyes in the car. I don't want to fall asleep.

The policeman tells me I am going somewhere where no one will hurt me.

***

I'm riding my bike. The chain got busted. I can't get home.

I must be dreaming.

I've gone too far. I don't know where I am.

I hear Mama yelling my name. She is standing in the door. It is all dark.

"Raymond! Ray Ray!"

I shout back, "Mama!"

The policeman tells me that I am dreaming. He tells me to be quiet and get some rest.

The door to my house shuts.

Raymond is returned to his home after the incident, and after the three days it takes to get a shelter-care hearing. His dad is in jail, and the court determines that his mother is competent to care for her son.

PAINT

Bright colored pots of fingerpaint dot the work table. Four children sit on the edge of their seats, some tipped forward on the legs of their chairs, fingers crooked and ready while the teacher gives instructions. "Each of you has an outline of a body in front of you. Use the paints to color your body in. Each color has a feeling. After you paint, you can share your feeling body picture with the rest of the class."

I watch the kids as they dip their fingers into the cool and colorful goo. Nykiah uses a popsicle stick, not sure she wants to touch the stuff. Her picture is all yellow and reds with a big smeared smile in red- and rainbow-colored buttons to represent the shirt she is wearing.

The children share the paint. "I need more blue. Do you have the red?" They look at me. I am lost in the pleasure of their painting. "Do you have anymore red?" they demand.

Raymond looks up at me. (I have been working with him for a few weeks in play therapy. I have been in close contact with his mother and have visited their home often.) Raymond says, "I need some more black."

He is blotting out his picture of himself with black. Underneath, some brown and white and blue is still visible. With each layer of black he applies, the picture turns a darker and darker gray until the body outline is no longer apparent. Now, the entire paper is soaked through in black and beginning to tear in places from the weight of the wet paint.

I get Raymond another pot of black and he applies the whole container to his already saturated picture obliterating any remaining structure or form. On the bottom edge is a glimmer of white border that has escaped his onslaught. I ask Raymond to tell me about his picture.

"This is me," he points with black tipped fingers. "Being a

bad boy," he adds. "Write that down." I write the caption: "This is me being a bad boy," on the margin of white at the bottom of the paper.

The next day, I take the picture, still wet in places, to Raymond's mother. She is sitting in the dark, in her white nurse's uniform, when I arrive. Since she has been clean, she has been working as an aid in a nursing home. A corridor of light comes in through the broken living room window and rests on her face.

Darlene is always welcoming when I come to her house. She often talks through tears. She wants a better life for her kids. She can't leave Ray's father because she needs what little is left over after he buys crack, to buy milk and bread for her kids. There is never enough money, even with her job, to buy her kids new shoes. Ray's toes poke holes through his high tops. Darlene looks extra tired today. I wish I hadn't brought the picture.

Raymond comes out to say hello to me. His mother sends him to his room. She thinks that is what I want, so we can talk. I tell her that it's okay, he can come out. I don't mind at all. She says this is our time to talk and leaves her son in his room.

I can't hide the picture. Darlene wants to see what I have rolled up under my arm.

I know why I have brought the picture. Darlene and I have talked so many times about Raymond's rages, the yanking out of his hair, his fear of his father, the way he has stopped attending at circle time, the time he got really mad and peed all over the walls and floor of the boys' bathroom. Darlene had made a fist and said, "You can be sure, he'll never do those things again." She wasn't getting it. That's why I brought the picture.

I lay the painting out on the coffee table. Although it is only three o'clock, the living room is dark. Darlene turns on a dim lamp.

"This is Raymond's self-portrait; please read the caption."

I watch Darlene as she reads each word slowly and then reads them again. "'This is me being a bad boy.'" She raises herself up on the sunken couch cushions and takes a closer look.

"The assignment," I say, "was for each child to fill in their body outline with different colors symbolizing feelings. This is what Ray painted."

Darlene starts to speak to me, but words don't come.

"Raymond," she hollers. "Come out her this minute." I am afraid she is going to strike the boy.

Raymond lingers in the hallway. His mother beckons to him and he runs to cradle himself in her lap. Her arms reach all the way around him. She understands.

BASKETBALL

The sessions go well. Ray is healing slowly by replaying the trauma he has experienced through the symbolic language of play. We're into our sixth session.

"Actually, my name isn't Raymond," he tells me straight off. "I am Shawn Kemp."

I have to think for a minute who Shawn Kemp is and then I remember buying this superstar's basketball jersey last year at a department store. I bought an extra-large for my oldest brother who also believes himself to be Shawn Kemp at times.

The playroom where Raymond and I meet has a bare tile floor except for a small, carpeted square in the northeast corner. We naturally gravitate to the carpeted area; that's where most of the toys are.

Ray Ray finds a torn up, plastic laundry basket and pieces it together, somehow, with his four-year-old fingers. We now have a basketball hoop. He sets the basket up on top of a five-foot high bookshelf.

It is February and the sun is coming through the windows from where it hovers outside above the schoolyard. Raymond has on blue shorts and a tank top that says, "Kool Kid," in bubble letters across his chest. When he props the laundry basket on top of the shelf, his biceps bulge. He is so skinny. All of his muscles and bones show through lustrous brown skin.

He finds a bunch of deflated tennis balls in the closet and our game begins. He is the boss.

"I'm Shawn Kemp," Ray Ray tells me. "You guard me." I think about getting on my knees to make the game fair, but while I am thinking, Ray lopes a basket right over my head from his self-imposed three pointer line.

"All right Raymond!" I exclaim.

Raymond stops dribbling and looks at me. "I am *not* Raymond. My name is Shawn. Shawn Kemp."

"Sorry Shawn," I apologize.

"Shawn" resumes play and I do my best to guard him, but he keeps popping tennis ball baskets, hooking and popping them in long arcs over my head. It isn't until he slam dunks a ball so hard that his forearm catches on a jagged edge of the plastic "hoop", that Shawn becomes Raymond again.

His arm is bleeding a little. Instantly, he collapses to the floor whimpering and holding his arm. He lets me take a look, and I see a small scrape just below the elbow, along the flat place of bone.

To Raymond, the scrape is not superficial. It brings with it every old wound that has been left unattended.

I get the first aid kit. I open a packet that contains a disinfectant towlette and dab at the sore spot. Ray winces, but allows me to continue. I make a big deal out of his scrape. I decide that a Band-Aid is too ordinary. This requires something special. Something that I can make more of a fuss over.

I open a new package of gauze and unroll a long strip. I squeeze out a drop of healing ointment from an old, tired tube and spread the goo on Raymond's arm. I cut two pieces of white, surgical tape and apply the gauze pad to the wound. The gauze smells fresh.

Ray Ray watches me with unbroken attention as I tend to his scrape. Afterward, I get him a little paper cup of water, and he drinks some of it sitting in my lap. I tell him how brave he is and what a great basketball player he is. He asks me to draw a picture of him as Shawn Kemp, to keep.

I look in drawers and closets and can't find any paper. I spot a box of crayons and a stack of brown paper lunch bags on an old desk that has been shoved into a corner of the room. I take a bag and begin to draw. I look at Raymond and then back at my drawing taking shape on the bag.

I draw Raymond taller with bigger muscles, but leave him in the clothes he is wearing — the shorts and the tank top. I change the color of his clothes to green and instead of writing "Kool

Kid," I write "Shawn Kemp," and the number "40" on his jersey. I give the finished drawing to Raymond and he grins a little.

We walk back to my office and Raymond insists on carrying my papers and a box of toys he has brought to the room. The things he carries are awkward and burdensome, but he refuses help. He can barely see over the box and stumbles once on the cracked asphalt.

Ray asks for my keys. He sets the box down and fits a key into the lock. He opens the door to my office. He asks me, "Do you have anything to eat?" I look around the office and I look in some cabinets. I find some packages of saltines and processed cheese. We sit on the floor, spread bright yellow cheese onto the crackers, and eat.

PLAY

The other stuff that Raymond and I play is "jail," "house," and "playground."

The way Raymond plays out jail is to turn it into a fun sort of place that has a swimming pool and coke and candy machines that his father can use at will. At first, jail with Ray takes on a kind of country club atmosphere. Later it turns into something else.

The first few sessions we go to the "jail" to visit Raymond's father, and then we help him escape. Not a high risk kind of escape, but an easy-does-it escape. We simply walk out of the jail with Ray's father and pack him into the waiting station wagon. This is only after we've swum in the Olympic size pool and sat in the hot tub eating chocolate bars to our hearts' content.

There are never any guards around. In these scenarios, Raymond's dad is always benevolent and kind.

The jail itself is an old cardboard refrigerator box I salvaged from the appliance store down the street. Ray gets in the box and becomes his dad. Before getting into the box, Ray makes sure to take a toy gun and the play telephone. Then he calls me up. I'm assigned the role of Raymond.

"Raymond," he says, "Do you think you could come on up here and visit me? Bring your bathing suit. There's a big pool."

I pretend to drive to the jail and right away Raymond emerges from his cell, pretending to be his dad, and gives me a wave. Then we swim in the pool, and he assigns me the role of his father and tells me to toss him into the air. Raymond pretends to splash in the water that is the dirty, old carpet in the playroom. We are always the only people at the jail.

After the swim, Raymond reverses our roles, and he is dad behind bars. I sit outside the jail box waiting while Raymond, in the role of his father, talks on the phone.

When he gets on the phone he becomes both himself and his dad, changing his voice to suit both roles. He repeats this play scene for several sessions. The conversation usually goes like this: "Be sure to bring your bathing suit," Ray says in a deep voice, and then: "Dad, can I get a Coke and some M&M's out of the machine?"

"Yeah [in the deep voice], but you got to bring your own money. A dollar will cover it."

Once we escaped jail, and returned home, Raymond would become his dad and make us the most delicious barbecued chicken in the world. I would play along, eating imaginary food off of plastic plates and licking imaginary sauce off of my fingers. Ray would say, "Do you want some more?" and I would answer, "Yes. This is the best chicken in the world."

We could play like this for an hour and, when the time ran out, it was hard to get back into our everyday roles. Me as therapist. Raymond as student, son, child of pain.

After one of our sessions, Raymond told me about his bike.

"The chain is busted and I can't go anywhere," he said.

I knew how important it was for Raymond to have his bike, a real vehicle of power and freedom. His mother would not have the money to fix it. I didn't want to shame her by taking care of the problem myself, but he pleaded with me. He knew that my neighbor loved bikes. "Do you think your friend could fix it?"

I called Darlene and she said it was okay for me to pick the bike up after work. She sounded exhausted, her voice slow and easy. She was beyond shame and said, "Yes. That would be fine. Yes."

Session Notes

Mar 27: Immediately asked for guns. Tried to kill the bad guy — didn't die. Asked for my help.

Left the guns on the floor and went to play with the shark in the sandbox. Filled the shark with sand. "The shark ate the bad guy, but he's still living in his stomach." Kept filling and emptying the shark with sand. Started talking about his dad. "When I'm sad and crying, my dad whips me. I don't like getting whipped."

Said his mom loves his dad. Asked me a lot of questions (i.e. Do I ever get whipped by my dad?)

Went back to the guns and started hunting bad guy. Asked me if I had ever been to jail. Stuck two guns in his belt. Played himself as the bad guy and shot me and the teddy bear.

Switches to my protector. Says, "Somebody was trying to bust in your door and it was your husband. He stayed outside. He was trying to wait for you to open the door."

Apr 3: Unfocused. Distracted. Hunting bad guy with gun. Then switches to himself (Ray) killing himself by shooting himself in the head. Falls to the floor dead. Gets up and puts on a black mask and kills me, shooting me over and over again.

Lots of talk about my house. "Can we go to your house?" Picks up the gun and "kills" playmate. Calls 911 and revives her. Play is agitated and disintegrated. Goes to the sandbox.

Picks up the shark. "The shark ate my eyes, ears, mouth, and nose. I can't see or talk."

Apr 10: Lines up a fortress of little cars around the dollhouse. Tells me that my children are inside and they can't get out. Asks me, "Can your friend fix my Powerwheel?"

Plays around with the cars, crashing them into each other and crashing them into the walls. Says, "I love my dad." Draws a picture of his dad, happy in jail (see file).

Plays "hunting the bad guy." Takes breaks in between this and playing house. Plays that he and I are married. "We sleep together in the same bed." I lie down on the floor next to Ray. "We are sleeping in the kitchen with our baby sister," he says. Then he throws the "baby sister," out of the house and says that she is my daughter and she doesn't belong in here. Gets up and gets the toy knives and stabs the girl. Calls 911. Comes back to lay down beside me.

Apr 17: Calls to me and says, "Surprise. I shoot out your eyes and mouth. I shoot your whole body out. You stole the money." Plays this theme over and over. Shows no interest in fixing me. Does not call 911.

Apr 24: Hides the play money under the floor of the play house. Continues to shoot and kill me for stealing the money. "Shot your mouth out — you can't talk. Shot your eyes out, you can't see." Very absorbed. Stays in the play house guarding his money for about twenty minutes.

Switches to being the good guy. Hunts for the bad guy who is trying to steal the money. Ignores me. Comes out of role for clean-up. Goes to the sandbox before he leaves the playroom. Makes the shark and the alligator fight. Buries the shark. "You go to jail," he says to the shark.

Comes over and hugs me. Draws a picture (See file). Tells this story about the picture: "There was a ghost behind him and he tried to look backwards and there was a little boy behind him, and he punched him and pushed him down. He was crying after he did it, and the boy was crying too. His mom told him to get the sugar so he could make tea, and he pushed him down. The boy was in the way. The bad guy invited us to his house. He has a family."

Summary: For several weeks Ray's play has been acting-out the scene with the dollar bill. He is hypervigilant, constantly looking over his shoulder for the "bad guy." Ray wears the sunglasses. He asks me to pin the sheriff badge on his shirt. He shoots the bad guy. Ray shouts at the imaginary figure, "You stole my dollar bill!" The bad guy keeps reappearing. He won't die.

May 1: Ray plays basketball. Pretends to be Shawn Kemp. Gets injured and lets me fix him up. More trusting.

Ray shoots himself. Tells me to call 911. "You be the doctor." I play rescue and fix him up with bandages. Ray hugs me and wants to sit in my lap. Ray wants to play house. "I love you. I come to your house. Then you come to my house." Ray stays close to me. Ray draws a picture of me (see file).

No mention of the bad guy. Less anxious today. More focused. Checks the sandbox and sees that the shark is still buried. "You stay there," he says to the shark.

May 8: Ray plays teacher. Tells me to draw a picture of something happy on the board. Next, I am the teacher. I tell Ray to draw a picture of something happy. He draws on a pad of paper. (see file) "I'm crying. You tell my mom. No, tell my dad."

Ray will not allow me to comfort him as "Dad." He reverses roles and becomes his dad comforting me. Ray hugs me and then goes off to buy me a gun. Returns from the corner of the playroom with the potato-shooting gun for me. He is wearing sunglasses and the pirate hat. He asks me to put the fake moustache on him. Then he takes his own gun and pretends to shoot himself.

May 15: Plays store. Buys himself a phone and a gun. Plays house. Cooks chicken for us. Then plays "baby" for much of the session. Finds a pacifier and sucks on it. Lets me hold him and rub his back. Lets me cover him with a blanket. Talks in baby talk. "I wan' mo baba." Cooks. I am Dad. He is Mom. Says, "I love you honey."

> Tenor of play changes. Police come to arrest Dad. They put him in the patrol car. "I didn't do nothin'... I didn't do nothin!" Ray yells. Ray helps Dad escape from jail with his mom's help. Shoots a policeman blocking their way.

JAIL

Eventually, Raymond was allowed a supervised visit with his dad at the jail. The goal: to eventually reunite the family and provide them with ongoing treatment. It wasn't clear who was going to pay for the ongoing treatment.

Darlene had come to see me at school after my visit to her home. She told me that she was going to take Raymond and go into hiding so that when big Ray got out of jail he would not be able to find them. I was not surprised, however, when a week later I found out that Darlene was the one who had pushed for visitation.

When Raymond came back from his first visit to the jail, the tenor of his play changed drastically. If he hadn't felt enough responsibility before for what had happened to his father, now he was consumed by guilt. He believed that his father's imprisonment directly related to his actions on the day of the "stolen" dollar bill incident. It didn't matter if he was stealing the dollar bill off of his father's dresser or just looking at it. Ray now blamed himself for his father's suffering. He told me, "My dad didn't do nothing wrong."

Our therapy back-tracked. Ray felt that he deserved the beating he had gotten and more.

Bad boy.

Raymond's play took on a decidedly aggressive tone. He chose to work with clay almost every session. He excluded me from his play. The themes he played out were around danger, death, annihilation, and entrapment.

In Raymond's world, four-drawer file cabinets can topple over and crush you. Men go to jail and, if they are too skinny, they disappear down the toilet without a trace. You wouldn't even know that they had ever existed. Larger men in jail get their stomachs cut in two with scissors. You could get hit by a car or suffocate to death like the rubberized shark that ate the miniature plastic bird cage, but those ways, Raymond tells me, would be too painful. He would prefer a single gunshot to the head.

The little green safety scissors get stuck in the clay, but Raymond yanks them out and pushes the blunt instrument through thick walls of clay, cutting and stabbing the figures he has created; men in jail, toilets made of putty, little groupings of clay men. No sisters or mothers, wives, or daughters.

In his play, Raymond is in jail and has made himself the tallest and strongest one by rolling several balls of brown and white clay into cylinders which he gloms together to form a torso that looks like the bound wooden pilings seen at ferry boat landings.

While Raymond is working I have made a blue hat out of soft clay and smoothed the brim with a tongue depressor borrowed from the nurse's office. Raymond likes the nurse and he likes the hat. He accepts the blue dome and places it on his clay head. The hat fits and he breathes out a smile of relief. "The hat is important," he tells me, "because the boy's mother made it." He does not cut the hat or smash it down, but removes it now and then from his clay head and places it gently on a nearby shelf.

Raymond tells me that his clay self is surrounded by a force field that stays with him through the day and night. In this way, he can do battle with the bad guy at a moment's notice. Instantly, one squat clay-figured bad guy fractures into three bad guys.

"Who is that one?" I ask pointing to a blob of clay formed into a figure.

"Another prisoner," says Raymond.

"What about that one?" I ask pointing to the other figure.

"That's the devil! He's my cell mate."

"I thought you shared your cell with your dad?"

"I told you! I sleep with the devil! The devil lives inside of everyone and the angel does, too."

"Which one lives most inside of you?"

"The angel," and Raymond smiles at me. His face looks eerie under the glow of the fluorescent lights. Raymond's front teeth are all crooked. He takes a sip of milk from the half-pint carton on the table and I can see that he is still a boy.

—— 📖 ——

The formica table top is littered with a number of slapped-together figures and one carefully made sabor-tooth tiger with huge brown fangs that overpower the animal's body, tipping it forward, the fangs bending under the pressure.

A border of Playdough fence borrowed from another child's work becomes the jail. Raymond fashions a toilet out of the modeling clay. I'm searching around for more clay. I look frantically in desk drawers, on the top of shelves and file cabinets. I look under the table for fallen pieces and notice wads of pink, gray, and green chewing gum stuck to the underside of the table. I think of all of the children who have sneaked and pressed their gum under the table.

I come back to Raymond. I want to fill him up and feed him with tremendous mountains of clay, but I have no more to offer.

Raymond hangs another prisoner by the neck in a loop of green clay attached to the body/piling figure that is his own. Raymond's softly sculpted head is popped on top of the pilings in the blue hat that I have made. Raymond has made himself armless and the noose dangles from his body like an unbuckled belt.

Raymond puts another prisoner in clay jail and then cuts him up and feeds his body parts to clay pets that other children have made.

"The pets like the head the best," he informs me, intent over his work. Raymond is careful to not destroy the things other children have made — penguins and robots, little goblins, dogs, pumpkins, and trees.

CHILD PROTECTIVE SERVICES

Today, the caseworker from Child Protective Services has come to the therapeutic child care center to investigate because there have been reports of Darlene hitting Raymond with her shoe, a piece of a toy racetrack, anything handy. Raymond has been coming to school with small blisters in the "V" between his thumb and first finger from heating his own frozen pizzas in the oven. Darlene is among the people who have called in a report to the authorities. "Please, just come and take my boy, for a little while," she sobbed into the phone. "I don't know why he is so angry. He is talking about killing himself. I am so afraid. Please help me." I suspect that Darlene is using again.

When the caseworker arrives at the center and steps into my office, Raymond is his clay. He does not notice this man who has entered the room and introduced himself as Terry.

Terry talks on and on at Raymond who dives deeper into his work. Raymond coats one pair of scissors in layers and more layers of supple white sculpting clay and stabs at his right hand until the end of the green plastic scissors pokes through and makes contact with his skin. "You're left handed," I observe and he grins.

"I got that way from when my other arm got broken. My mom gave me a lot of presents then. If I broke my leg she might give me some more stuff."

The caseworker looks at his notes and fires off a long list of impossible questions: "What did you have for dinner last night? Do you know what drugs and alcohol are? Does anyone in your house put those things into their body? What did your daddy go to jail for?"

Raymond ignores the questions, and I see Terry note something on his clipboard. Raymond goes to the wall and picks off the rabbit mask. Before putting it on, he fills the mask with small bits of multi-colored clay that have come together out of the chaos on the table.

Terry tells Raymond that he's worried about him.

"It says right here," he notes looking at his file, "that you've talked about killing yourself. Is that true?"

"Yeah!" Raymond shouts zig-zagging across my small office in precise lines as if on a tight-rope. "Yah, I'll tie myself to the electric garage door and boom! That will be the end of me. My dad told me to get out of his life."

"I hear that your dad used to beat you up quite a bit. Is that true?" asks Terry.

"Yeah. Like this and like this!" Raymond strikes at the air, his skinny arm weighted by the ball of his fists and demonstrates punching.

"And I hear that you are hitting other children at school. Is that true?" Terry asks.

"You mean the devil," yells Raymond. "I'm killing the devils."

I toss Raymond a teddy bear: "Pretend this is David — show me what you do." Raymond claws at the bear and presses his hands around its neck until his knuckles turn white. The other day his teacher had come upon him choking another classmate like this.

"This worries me — all this fighting," says Terry.

"I could drown myself, too, or get everyone out of the building and then blow myself up with T and T," Raymond announces.

Terry says, "I'm worried about you, Ray."

Raymond makes stabbing gestures with the scissors into his stomach and heart. He takes a sip of milk and a bite of apple. "I could poke myself to death," he shouts to no one in particular.

Terry tells Raymond that he has already talked to his mother.

I know what Terry had said in response to Darlene's plea for help for herself and her son, the usual script: "I really think you need to finish your job training, lay off the drugs and the booze, take a parenting class, get some counseling."

Last week Raymond told me that his eyes are the same color as his mother's, hazel, and that they turn all sorts of different colors when he cries. He tells me that he cries every day.

Terry leaves and says he'll be back tomorrow to interview Raymond again. I am afraid Raymond may be dead by then.

Raymond ignores Terry and pleads with me, "Can I please come back down here tomorrow?" He looks so small. This four year old with enough anger to blow up the whole city.

I glance at my calendar. I feel ashamed. Suddenly, my well-ordered life appears frivolous, ridiculous. I say, "I'll make time for you," without looking at my schedule.

Raymond leaves and I am left alone with a table full of dull-colored clay pieces that have all gone mute.

I start sorting; the washed-out blues together, the greens together, the faded yellows together. I do not take apart anything made whole.

A tiny Japanese flag rests on a broken toothpick. Its stem splintered into a jagged spear from when Raymond tried to jam it into a clay penguin. He had looked at me then, his eyes wide with fear and surprise, and I had said, "You're not in trouble."

Later that day, Darlene calls me. She says that Child Protective Services has been out at her house. She asks me how come I didn't tell her they were coming. She is not angry; she sounds scared. "I think they may take my boy away." She starts to cry.

I tell her, "Everything will be all right." I don't think that this is true. I don't know what will happen, so I just tell her to try and relax. I'll talk to Terry tomorrow.

Darlene pleads with me, "Please don't let them take my boy again." Some of her words slur. She is drunk or high or both. I wonder if Raymond is listening.

Raymond doesn't get taken from his mother this time. The system doesn't work that fast. It is too hard for most people to believe that a four year old can be depressed and suicidal. It is easier to see when a child is hungry, or dirty, or has been smacked around too much. But Raymond's mother doesn't get the help that she needs either. Breaking the attachment of parent/child can be more damaging than removing a child from a dangerous home life. It is a tough call. The physical safety of the child versus the emotional bonds that are essential to healthy development.

Terry doesn't come to my office the next day as promised. He calls and tells the secretary to tell me that he has some "emergency situations to take care of."

I continue to see Raymond in play therapy and, although he is far from healed, he begins to stabilize slowly. He will need much more care than I can give him.

Session Notes

May 22: Low energy. Played ball for awhile halfheartedly. Set out toy dishes for us to have a picnic. Lost interest. Preoccupied. Tells me, "My mom says we are moving."

Plays jail. Calls me (his wife) to bring him (Dad) a phone, toys, the doctor kit, and bathing suits. Plays role of Dad in jail. "I don't like it here." Takes toy gun and shoots himself in the head.

Looks tired. Says he is hungry. Tells me he is moving again. Plays jail. He plays the cops and gets me out. Says, "She didn't do nothin'." I tell him, "But I did do something. I hurt my little boy." Ray says, "That's O.K.."

Depressed. Playing out guilt at Dad's imprisonment. Worried about moving.

Concerned about me. "You was tryin' to get in the door and you ask your mom to go in the front door and that was locked. And you were good at tryin' to get in because there was a choo choo train and you got hit."

May 29: Regressing. Plays baby almost all the time now. Won't talk about moving. Drawings are scribbled. Wants me to be Dad taking care of the baby.

Digs the shark out of the sandbox. Backs up to me for a hug. Brings me a gift — a small box of chocolates. Won't eat one when I offer it. Says they are moving tomorrow. Just him and his mom and his brothers. Scribbles out a picture for me in red.

An End

T OWARD THE END OF MY TIME AT KID'S PLACE, I REALIZE THAT MY heart will be broken many times if I am to continue to do this work. I don't think that you can do the work well without becoming attached to your small clients, but to go too deeply within them or within yourself does not allow for healing.

After Ray Ray didn't show up anymore because our predetermined number of sessions ended, I became depressed and despondent. The amount of time necessary to rebuild a life appeared to be hopelessly long to me. So many children and families were left dangling in the middle of treatment because the funding dried up or they didn't have transportation to get the services they needed. I was tired all the time. I felt the same cold detachment I had criticized others for. For each troubled child I helped, I felt like there were a million more out there in the same or worse condition.

With Ray Ray, I felt I had just begun my journey into my own childhood memories. We were different in so many ways and yet we shared a certain vulnerability. The things he taught me stayed dormant until later when I began to work at Whitman Children's Home with adolescents and preadolescents, and I had a chance to look back at my life with some perspective. It was at this time that I began to question my attraction to this work. I became more confused and arrested in my own emotional development as I was exposed to older children who had and continued to experience difficult childhoods. It would take me years before I would confront my own need for healing and seek the help that I needed through therapy.

I remember one of my professors in graduate school talking about the importance of going through your own therapy in order to be a good therapist. Despite my belief in therapy for others, I didn't think it would work for myself. I worked for years at Whitman before I began to seek my own healing in a purposeful way — as purposeful as the work I did each day with the children and families I saw in treatment.

PART II

LOVE MUST BE LEARNED

*"Love must be learned, and learned again and again;
there is no end to it. Hate needs no instruction,
but only wants to be provoked."*
–Katharine Anne Porter

Group Home

I AM THIRTY-ONE YEARS OLD AND A GRADUATE STUDENT IN psychology when I start my job at Whitman Children's Home. A friend at school has suggested I take the job and see what the older kids are like. I quit my job at Kid's Place and begin work at Whitman, a residential treatment center for children age six to sixteen.

Whitman Children's Home is a wooded haven situated just east of a freeway. I imagined it to be a lot like Hillcrest, where my childhood friend Regina had lived — something like a modern day orphanage.

On the outside, Whitman looks like an estate, of sorts, for unwanted children. The grounds are well taken care of by a team of gardeners. Several "cottages" are set in between a spacious green lawn to the south and ravine of forest dropping off to the north. The large timbered dwellings cost a half a million dollars a piece and house twelve children.

On the inside, Whitman looks like a ski lodge. The front door opens to higher-than-cathedral ceilings, exposed wood posts and beams, and a blanket of unblemished russet carpeting. The only thing missing is a fireplace.

At Whitman, I feel constantly on the look-out for danger, which is clinically called hypervigilance. My palms sweat profusely and my heart races whether the kids are breaking windows or watching a video. I am always prepared for the worst. My brain circuits have well traveled pathways from the amygdala to the prefrontal lobes. The amygdala is the primitive, "emotional brain." It reacts in micro seconds to the slightest threat or thought of what it has learned to perceive as dangerous. To me, that could be a sneeze or a look in someone's eye. The message races to the more stable prefrontal lobes, where they try to reason with the emotional brain, but they don't always win and I can end up flooded, much like a car becomes flooded when the gas pedal is repeatedly slammed to the floor.

I realize that I have felt these bodily sensations for as long as I can remember. When I go through my own therapy later, I learn that my response to danger has been hard-wired in my brain from early childhood experiences. Although my history varies from the children that I work with, there are some similarities: sounds of overharsh discipline of my older brothers during the tulmultous years of the '70s. A mentally ill, older brother who sexually abused me for years. All this became imbedded in my brain and hardwired my nervous system. Early childhood trauma yields certain universal effects on most children that carry over into their adult life.

At Whitman, I believe that if I can just love the kids enough, they will heal. I am becoming aware at this time that I have my own healing to do in relation to these damaged children. At the time, I don't know how much my past is impacting my present. I don't know why I feel anxious and depressed much of the time. I believe that I have picked this profession of working with abused and neglected kids because I care so much. I believe that I can make a difference. I don't realize that my caring and needing to make a difference are diagnostic in themselves. I know that I was exposed to violence and mental illness in my own family, but knowing this and knowing the children I work with are like two parallel lines in space that never meet. It is only years later, when I get myself into therapy, that the lines meet and form a whole.

＊ 📖 ＊

My three-to-eleven shift at Whitman gives me plenty of flooding, but my body is strong and I am an expert at maintaining a calm exterior while, inside, my body wreaks havoc.

On my first three-to-eleven shift, I am greeted by a thirteen-year-old girl. "Who the hell are you?" she asks when I walk in the door. Janine looks more like sixteen than thirteen. Her hair is stiff with hair spray. It looks like it has been dyed and the color hasn't taken right. Janine's hair looks orange. She wears frosted pink lipstick, a tight, black mini-skirt, and eyes heavily made up with thick khol eyeliner and mascara.

Janine is sent to time out by another staff for being rude to me.

Another boy of eight or nine is already in time-out, slumped into an overstuffed chair in the corner of the main room, his blond hair catching rays of southern exposure from the floor to ceiling windows.

(I think it is too bad that my brother couldn't have gone to a place like this as a way station to the mental hospitals he now frequents. But we didn't know then, when he was a kid, that he was growing a psychosis that would explode into a monster one day.)

Whitman is a beautiful place, yet the kids are bored stiff. They do all kinds of things to break the monotony including cutting on their wrists and strewing garbage all over the living room carpet.

One kid urinates so much at night that the pee soaks through his mattress all the way down to his bed frame and rots the wood. Staff put his mattress on the floor and the pee soaks through some more and into the floor boards.

Janine cuts on her wrists and gets put on suicide watch. Frank goes home on a weekend pass and drives his mother's car off a cliff. The death is listed as an accident.

At Whitman the kids have to earn everything and so there's a lot of waiting time. It takes a long time to earn enough points to get on the hierarchy of privilege.

The kids at Whitman aren't little and they aren't cute anymore. They are adolescents or preadolescents whom nobody wants to adopt. A few adoptions went through during the year I was there, but most of them failed, and the kids were returned to Whitman to await another placement.

While the kids wait to pass the time, they daydream a lot or become destructive. Rhonda does both. She believes she is a ballet dancer and gets me to drive her to dance class on Saturday mornings.

Rhonda is overweight from eating institutional food and sitting around and watching television, but she doesn't seem to care. She dresses in sweats and a T-shirt and takes her place at the barre.

After a few weeks of lessons, Rhonda puts on a show for the children and staff of the cottage. She pops a cassette into a tape player and twirls and prances around the room in a pair of black tights and a red crop top. Her belly hangs over the tights and vibrates every time she jumps. Eventually, Rhonda gets dizzy and starts ricocheting off of the posts in the living room. She snags a toe on the carpet, but keeps going until the tape runs out. The music sounds tinny. It is obvious to the audience that Rhonda is improvising the whole time. The kids start to snicker and make rude comments under their breath. Staff give them warnings, but struggle to hold back their own laughter.

After Rhonda is finished she collects her tape player and goes to the kitchen. I think she is getting a glass of water, but she is getting out the kitchen scissors that have been left in a drawer by accident.

Rhonda retreats to her room, heaving and sweating. She takes the scissors and hacks off her hair with the kitchen scissors. Then she swings her cabbage patch doll by the legs and breaks her bedroom window with the doll's head.

Shelly

S HELLY COMES TO LIVE AT WHITMAN WHEN I AM STILL NEW AND unsure. I've had the job as residential counselor for about three weeks when she arrives.

Shelly has short spiky hair and a tough, tomboyish look to her. Her clammy hands seek protection in the pockets of my jeans, and she clings to me, pressing her head into my breasts. Shelly's eyes are all iris, muddy brown. It seems like there are no defining pupils. She has sour breath made from the ashes of worry.

Shelly's parents write to her at Whitman:

The Lord is Thy Shepherd. Do not forget to pray to Him. To make you better, you must pray harder. God helps those who help themselves. To heal yourself of your sins, you must entrust all your heart and all your soul in the Lord. It is the only way! Only then will you be able to come home. Mommy and Daddy love you so! You will always be our little girl.

—⬥— 📖 —⬥—

When Shelly lived at home, the rim of a coffee can ringed her bottom red when she sat to relieve herself in the corner of her bedroom. The humiliation of this act was forced upon her by the need to go. Eggshells lined the bottom of the can. She didn't want to talk about the eggshells in the can.

Shelly knew what the tape was for. A piece of masking tape about two inches long, taped high on the outside of the door frame, connected to the door. No strong lock to leave out the possibility of doing wrong. The temptation to open the door was always there like the rush of standing on the edge of a cliff, imagining what it would be like to jump. The tape so flimsy, with the power of a grenade. Once tripped, no turning back. Her parents would know that she had left her prison. Shelly's world would explode into bits.

Shelly's parents follow the doctrine of the Church: "Cayenne pepper is recommended for disobedience. It can be used for shirking chores, bad report cards, body odor. Rx: One teaspoon administered orally."

For Shelly, the rubber hose is Church. Her memory is of the hose, green and speckled with a golden ribbed opening. The priest wields the hose like a cobra. The fat boy in Shelly's Sunday School class (who is now also at Whitman) gets beaten with the rubbery tube. The other children watch. Shelly laughs.

Suddenly, the hose is turned on her. Water oozes from the mouth of the tube drenching the girl. Her frilly dress sticks to her ribs and you can see her nipples through her soaked undershirt.

— 📖 —

Shelly liked to brush my long brown hair. She giggled and brushed with great care. When she finished, she hugged and squeezed me from behind with a baby's longing. Then she nestled into my lap, playing with my nose and lips and hair — tracing my face like a map she had just found, guiding her way in the contours of flesh and bone.

Thanksgiving

I DIDN'T FEEL LIKE WORKING, BUT I HAD NOWHERE ELSE TO GO. THE staff were taking out the kids, who didn't get home visits to the Royal Fork Buffet, an all-you-can-eat place.

Shelly couldn't decide what to wear. When I came on shift, clothing was strewn over the furniture and cluttering the steps up to the girls' hall. Shelly was in a battle with one of the staff. "Fuck you! Fuck you! I'm not going. You can't make me get dressed." Shelly pounded on the floor and pulled at her hair, grabbing the short ends in fistfuls of rage.

The letters from Shelly's parents arrived regularly, once a week, gilded in red and gold with large exclamation points the size of raindrops. The words were made of round, chubby letters all puffed up and bloated. The words floated on the page like pond scum:

> *We love you darling baby girl. The Lord is with you, but you must honor him by praying ceaselessly day and night to rid you of the evil that abides within! Mommy and Daddy wait for you. We wait and wait! All we can think of is getting our little girl back. You must listen only to God! The people there are not CHRISTIANS! Remember who your true friend is. Jesus Christ. He is watching you and marking your sins! So always be a good girl and then you will come home soon into our waiting arms!*
>
> *In Jesus' name, Mommy and Daddy.*

Zach

FTER A FEW MONTHS AT WHITMAN, I AM PHYSICALLY restraining kids when they try to break a window, run off the grounds or punch another child square in the face. I become numb. I drive home at eleven o'clock at night exhausted. I swear out loud in the car as I drive, releasing words that have penetrated into my brain for eight hours: *fuckin' bitch, fuck you, fuck off, cunt.*

I try to relax my neck during the seven-mile trip to my one bedroom apartment. I roll my neck from side to side. I scrunch my shoulders up to my ears, then release them with a firm downward pull. I remember that I am not breathing deeply or evenly. My breath comes in short spurts from my upper chest. I try to force the air down through my stomach and into my abdomen. I feel like there is a horizontal line dividing my chest from the rest of me. The only thing I notice is my heart. My heart feels constricted like it has been anaesthetized. I am afraid for the sting of pain that will inevitably come when the numbing wears off. I make a mental note to keep my heart numb. I swear some more and let the events of the evening run through me. My memory already fails me. Was it Brian who threw the dart at Bruce or was it Jackson? My poor memory assures me that my heart will stay numb. I am so tired. I focus on the taillights in front of me.

The streets are dark without much movement, except for the silent journey of the car in front of me. The stillness frightens me. I search the night for signs of danger. My entire consciousness is programmed to be on the look out for danger.

Kids at Whitman are physical. They are violent, actually. They are primal in their expression of anger and fear. They strike out when cornered. They kick and scratch and scream an anger so embedded it takes that much force to shake it loose.

The kids at Whitman don't know how to trust or how to love. When people come too close, they shut down or act out. I played tennis with Zach for two months during the sunny months of July and August. I was sure that I was earning his trust. I was sure that he was learning to love.

Zach jumped me one night as I was doing night checks. The same kid that called me "ma'am," during his intake interview, sprang from behind his door like a panther and pounced on me. He was wearing only boxer shorts and his chest was a washboard of muscle. Zach was only eleven, but he got me down and pounded all over me. I tried to protect my head with my arms. Then I tried to contain him by holding onto his arms. That was like trying to hold onto the blades of a fan.

Zach scratched and scratched at my forearms until they bled. The other staff on duty was a woman. The male staff that night had called in sick. I called for Anna, and she came running. All the other kids were out of their beds and watching from the stairs. Both Anna and I did not have enough of what Zach had to stop his attack. When Anna could see that this was a losing battle she yelled to one of the kids to call the other cottage and get a man over here and quick. The child did not move.

Anna left me on the ground with Zach and got the phone herself. I could hear her shouting from downstairs. "We need a man at Cottage 4 and now!" In seconds, Frank was over, taking the steps to the downstairs boys floor three at a time. He broke up our fight. My fear and anger and love were all mixed up. This child could not be the same boy I had played tennis with for months. But it was the same child who had been locked in a dark closet as a baby while his mother prostituted in the one room they rented. It was the same child who came into the world addicted to heroin. It was the same child who had welts from beatings with the buckle end of the belt and was forced to perform sex acts with his uncle.

Frank contained Zach, but the next morning, his bed was empty. Frank didn't know the usual punishment for Zach when he went out of control was to strip him down to his jockeys and remove all the clothing from his room so that he couldn't run away. Zach ran.

We didn't see Zach for two more weeks. The police brought him back. He had been living on the streets downtown.

When Zach returned to Whitman the male staff took all the boys to the gym to play "soak 'em." This game involved throwing balls at each other from across lines that divided staff versus kids in teams. The staff became gladiators and pummeled Zach at close range with footballs and softballs.

By the end of the game, Zach was crying. The staff brushed the dust off of their clothes and returned to the cottage like triumphant warriors. The two male staff returned with the boy and announce to me, "We paid back Zach for you."

Lani

IT WAS LANI'S BIRTHDAY. KIDS AT WHITMAN WERE ALLOWED TO choose a staff to go out to dinner with them on their birthday. Lani chose me.

Lani had been playing on the "slip and slide" most of the afternoon. The slip and slide is a sheet of plastic that we turned the garden hose on. The kids got their bathing suits on and ran, fell, and slid along the wet plastic. The temperature was in the nineties, and the kids were bored and irritable so Shelly suggested the slip and slide, and the staff was happy to have the kids out of their way for awhile.

Lani talked to the other girls about getting to go out to dinner with me. Rhonda was especially jealous. Lani was up to slide. The ends of her short hair were dripping water and her bathing suit sagged where it was too big in the seat.

Rhonda couldn't wait her turn. Lani ran and slid. Rhonda was on her heels. In an instant, Lani was swearing in Rhonda's face. "You fuckin' cunt. You stuck your foot up my ass. How would you like it if I stuck my foot up your ass?"

The two girls were in a fight tugging at each other's hair and flailing wildly as the hose ran over their bare feet, water puddling in the muddy grass. When I went to break up the fight, Rhonda gave up quickly not wanting a consequence. But Lani wouldn't let up. She lunged at Rhonda after I had separated the girls. She repeated, "How would you like it if I stuck my foot up your ass?"

I kept telling Lani that she needed to get control. It was her birthday, and I knew how she had been looking forward to our

67

dinner for weeks. Lani shouted at me to "Shut up." She was beyond all reason. Her skinny body shook with rage and tears poured down her wet cheeks. I sent her to her room to cool off. Lani stormed through the cottage ripping artwork off the walls. She slammed the door to her room and began flinging things around. The other staff on duty said, "Well, I guess she's just blown her dinner out with you."

I knew that Lani's behavior was unacceptable, but I also knew that she had lived with her family in a car for over a year, near the migrant camps in Eastern Washington. Her father had repeatedly molested her. She was ten years old when she came to Whitman and eleven by the time I left. No one wanted to adopt Lani.

I didn't care what Lani had done. She deserved a night out for her birthday dinner. I was heartbroken when the supervisor wouldn't budge on her decision to give Lani an alternate consequence. She didn't get the night out. I don't know where she is now or whatever happened to her.

Rhonda's Point of View

*A*t Whitman Children's Home we wait for everything. I figure this is to put us into a dependent position. That way we're easier to control. They don't give out meds here, just warnings, restrictions, and earned privileges. You practically got to earn enough points to take a dump. There's this thing called, "a token economy." Some guy found out that if you give a pigeon a pellet every time the bird does what you want, he'll do more of it — or something like that.

We wait for enough points to earn an outing. That can take a long time if you blow it and get put on watch. We wait for lunch, which is always late. We stand in line at the door of the staff room for toothpaste and toothbrushes, pens and pencils and rulers and help with our homework. We wait for someone to want us.

I hate it when I have to ask for stuff. I feel so small like no one trusts me with anything. If I wanted to kill myself I could think of a lot of other ways than waiting in line for a pair of scissors. Sharon told me it's 'cause they're worried we may try and kill ourselves with sharp objects, cords, or even dental floss. You know someone actually did kill themselves by saving up dental floss and making a noose in some prison.

Sharon is so quiet, the oldest one here, maybe sixteen. She sits around in her bathrobe all day and never smiles. She is nice to the younger kids and staff don't seem to bother her, she keeps to herself pretty much. At night when the graveyard falls asleep, Sharon comes into my room late at night and talks about killing herself. She looks so frail and small. Usually her eyes are red from crying when she comes. I try to cheer her up with a stashed candy bar. She'll only take a bite.

The older girls get their private things one at a time in a paper lunch sack. I hope that I'm out of here before I have to do that. Janine doesn't care. She called you a "bitch" on her first day and yelled at the top of her lungs, "I need a plug!" She got sent to her room for two hours.

Shelly has been at Whitman for a year, just a little less time than me, and she still hasn't learned to suck up properly. She came here just before her eleventh birthday, all skinny and gawky looking with freckles and spiked hair. Pretty radical for coming from a Christian family.

It was cold the day Shelly came. Rain beat on the windows and all of us were bored stiff. I think just about the whole cottage was on some degree of restriction or another that day and so when the new girl arrived it was big time excitement.

The community service officers blew into our family room with their ugly brown uniforms, no guns. They're too wimpy to handle guns, I smirked as I watched them struggle with Shelly digging her heels in at the door as she refused to go any further. "What the hell?" she screamed. "They've put me in a fucking hunting lodge."

These so-called cottages we live in are really million dollar buildings with high tech alarm systems and prison yard type lighting. They stuck them out in the woods away from the rest of civilization so we wouldn't contaminate the rest of the world or anything.

Shelly refused to come in. She sat in the doorway with her knees up to her chest and planted her high-heeled cowboy boots into the carpet. The three staff on, Larry, Anna, and you, the new one, just watched. Shelly didn't know who she was messing with with Larry on. Anna and you, she could have gotten away with this shit, but I saw Larry's fingers curling and his chest heaving. In a matter of seconds he had the girl on the floor face down and was sitting on her back. "Now we'll see who's boss," he said. I saw the carpet had a big run in it from where Shelly's boots had caught and snagged. It would take Larry a little while to think of a good punishment for that one.

Shelly and I are the last ones of the original group who haven't been adopted yet. We are what some people call "throw-away children." Too old to hold any charm for adoption, too young to be out on our own. We've become best friends, and now she's leaving before me. I've stopped eating because of it, but no one seems to notice, not even you.

Ever since Shelly got hurt the staff started speeding up her adoption proceedings. They never said that was why, but all of a sudden she's going to her aunt's like hell bent for leather.

I can't wait to get out of this place. I wait in line to pee and brush my teeth and take a shower. I wait for shift change at seven a.m. and three and again at eleven p.m. to see who's on.

You started the night Shelly came. I didn't think you'd last long. Too pretty. Too scared. (Janine says you're a whore.)

Janine is big for her age and wears tons of makeup out of this little suitcase she keeps under her bed. Staff removed the little scissors and tweezers. Janine has a loud mouth. I can tell she has it in for you because she's jealous. She sees the way male staff look at you.

Janine dumped the kitchen garbage all over the living room floor when you asked her to empty it. Then she just stood there and waited for you to do something. You got all quivery and looked like you were going to cry. Your face was bright red. Larry had to intervene. He's the worst. Janine did what he said when he grabbed her arm and yelled into her ear, "Pick up this shit!" You're gonna have to get way tougher if you're gonna last. You've got to last!

The boys live on the downstairs floor. There's Jackson with his old man's face, looks like he's at least ninety years old, and Brian who runs away all the time, and Bruce. He's always playing with himself. It's disgusting. Sometimes he does it right out in the open and doesn't even cover himself. A real pervert. Rumor has it he's been jerking off more since you started.

When it rains, we play basketball together under the covered roof and the game always ends up in a big fight. Zach broke my finger once. We told staff we were just roughhousing, that it was an accident and in a way it was, even though I knew Zach meant to do it at the time. He's like a Doberman, so tough and skinny and quick. He ran that night — same as after he jumped you behind his bedroom. He doesn't like to hurt people. Can't help himself sometimes.

Since Shelly came, things have been better for me. She's only mean when people corner her or call her "boy." She does look like a boy, a little tomboy. We're roommates. Carol left and Shelly got the empty bed. At first her B.O. bothered me because she wouldn't take showers, and Larry threatened to have the woman staff hose her down outside in the dead of winter. You were the one who got her to wash. You were the only one who bothered to find out that Shelly had had plenty of cold hose showers in her life and would be happier in a tub bath.

Shelly and I talk about what we're going to do when we're free. We stay up late and talk about running away to live in the woods in a lean-to and cook meals over a fire. Good food like hamburgers and steaks and big bowls of ice cream and all the candy we can hold. The problem is we don't have any money.

You never know who's going to adopt you. Me? No one has come for me. I can't believe Shelly is going before me. If we couldn't run we were going to try to go together, but no one wants two girls. Shelly's only leaving so quick because she got hurt. I don't think her aunt really wants her. They're probably paying her off big time.

Shelly's parents punished her with teaspoons full of raw cayenne pepper so when one of the staff, Randy, made a joke that we would be having cayenne pepper with dinner, Shelly left the table and balled up in a corner of the living room.

Letters from Shelly's parents come once a week at least. They're so twisted. "We miss you. God loves you," and all that shit.

After her second month at Whitman, Shelly earned enough privilege points to come with us to the ballet one night. She was more fascinated with the plushed-out bathrooms of the Opera House than the ballet.

At intermission, Shelly spent a half an hour in the red velvet of the ladies room while she barked like a dog and scurried over the cushions sniffing while dressed up ladies washed their hands and dried them and pretended not to notice what was going on in the reflection of the mirrors.

On Easter, Shelly couldn't decide what to wear. She was twelve and clothes were important, more important than anything else at the time. The few clothes she had bought on the bullshit clothing voucher had lost their magic. She wanted something new. There was nothing. She tried to borrow Lani's fuzzy green sweater. Lani said, "You'll slobber on it."

Shelly began pacing the hall of the girl's floor. Her voice rang out shrill through the cottage. "I can't wear anything. I can't go. I have nothing to wear." She began to race. Foamy bits of spit collected at the corners of her mouth. She bolted downstairs to the staff office and demanded something to wear. Shelly burst into the staff room without permission. She had become more animal than girl. She tore at your face, swept papers off your desk and ripped them with her hands and teeth. I tried to tackle her to the floor and hold her but you shoved me aside. I had never seen you so pumped up.

72

You held Shelly tight between your legs with your arms crossed and folded over her chest, your legs over Shelly's. Shelly thrashed around and tried to bite you. I didn't say a word. You held her forehead back with one hand. Sobs broke from inside Shelly and welled up in these huge waves of grief. It sounded like she was choking, and I felt my own throat tighten.

Then, all of the sudden Shelly went limp like someone had let all the air out of her and she and you cried together and looked a little surprised to find that you were now in an embrace, with Shelly's flushed cheek and spike hair resting against your chest.

I felt jealous, but now I knew you'd stay awhile.

In bed that night, I asked Shelly what it felt like to be so near to you. I wanted to know what you smelled like and what it felt like to be held in your arms.

For weeks after the ballet, Shelly didn't get into trouble. I guess she liked getting out that much, saw that it was really worth working for. But one night when flower smells came in through our open window and the days became lighter and longer, Shelly decided that she wasn't ready to go to bed. Larry, Randy, the newest staff, and you were on that night.

I went up and started getting ready when Larry bellowed, "Ten minutes till lights out, ten minutes." I noticed Shelly standing by the carved wooden pillar and signaled with my eyes to "come on." She gave me a cold stare that she normally reserved for staff. I couldn't figure what had got into her. We were on the list for a hike in a few days. I was counting on Shelly to come. I lingered on the steps willing her with all my might to come, but she wouldn't budge.

"What are you lookin' at?" Randy asked me. "Move it." I turned and went up the steps to the girls' floor hoping Shelly would be right behind me. I called Randy a dick under my breath.

"Lights out," Larry yelled and Shelly was still not in bed. I heard you going from room to room checking on all the girls. You let me read with a flashlight. You were cool. I tried to concentrate on my book, but I kept wondering what the heck Shelly was doing. She hadn't been like this for weeks. I listened and it was quiet except for the new leaves of spring rubbing together in the breeze outside my window.

You padded down the stairs and I saw you settle into a staff chair with a cone of light from the high ceilings surrounding your head in a warm glow, like a little halo.

I tried to stay awake for Shelly, but I kept drifting in and out of sleep. It made me feel good to know that you would be on until eleven.

I started up thinking I was in a dream. Shelly was thrashing and screaming unintelligible words all jumbled together.

From my bed I could see down the hallway, and I saw arms flailing and the bodies of Randy and Larry trying to hold Shelly. It wasn't a dream. I could hear little pieces of what Shelly was saying, "Get off a me. Pervert. You animal. Fuckin' scum bag." This was gonna cost her.

A chair flew across the room, but I couldn't tell who threw it. Larry was shouting warnings, "You'll get a month's early beds for this and restriction, too." I couldn't hear Randy, but all of a sudden it got real quiet and there was no crying or shouting or movement and you had long since disappeared from your chair. I saw the office door close. I waited for almost an hour straining to see and hear in the dark before you brought Shelly upstairs, helped her undress and tucked her into bed. I waited for you to leave, pretended I was asleep. When you left the room it smelled like lavender.

"Shelly," I whispered. " What was that? What? Tell me."

Shelly started to cry. "Just a fight. It was nothin'. I told Randy I knew ... I knew all along he's been fuckin' Sharon every night he's on. I told him to his face, the big fuckin' baby."

— 📖 —

The next morning was Saturday. We were all allowed to sleep in as long as we wanted so I knew something was wrong. Normally, we were up by eight thirty on a weekend. Shelly was not in bed when I woke up. The office door was shut again, and you were back for morning shift even though you weren't on the schedule until Monday. Randy who was on the schedule was gone. An idiot could have figured this one out.

Shelly woke up early. She told me; "I'll be leaving in two weeks. I guess my aunt wants me after all."

I felt myself sink into a hole that I knew I would never be able to climb all the way out of.

"You can't leave me. Please. You can't go."

"It's already arranged."

We talked for hours and cried and hugged and Shelly promised she would write and get her aunt to take me too. "It'll be okay," she said staring out the window. The wind lifted her hair and I saw the red marks. The fingers of bruises around her slender neck.

I couldn't help myself, "Shelly. What the..."

She looked startled out of a dream world. "What?"

"What's with your neck, that's what?"

Shelly put her hand to her neck and shrugged.

"It's a rug burn," she said, "that's all, just a rug burn from last night."

Shelly left as scheduled two weeks to the day, and Randy returned from vacation, showing off his tan in a tight little muscle shirt.

He acted worse than ever ordering everyone around and eating his takeout dinners of hamburgers and shakes at the table in front of us while we ate macaroni and cheese. I couldn't stand to look at him or go near him. Sharon had given up her single room and moved in with me when Shelly left. She was more depressed than ever. I prayed every night that she would stay alive.

PART III

THE ROAD BACK

"The road was new to me,
as roads always are coming back."
–Sarah Orne Jewett

Burnout

AFTER ELEVEN MONTHS, I QUIT WHITMAN. I LIVE OFF OF MY savings and attend graduate school in psychological counseling.

One day I'm broke and feeling low, so I make an appointment at the beauty school. For half the price of a regular salon, they will color, shampoo, cut, and dry my hair. This will take twice as long as in a regular salon.

My date for a haircut is on a Saturday afternoon in October — a date with "Destiny." I call the place, and that's what she says when she answers the phone: "My name is Destiny and I will be your person."

I feel overwhelmingly tired. I look inward and find no answers. I start to look to my exterior. Maybe it's my hair, or I need to lose a few pounds. I scrutinize myself in the mirror. I look into the bathroom mirror of my studio apartment. I lean on my elbows and study my face, smoothing my fingers over imperfections. I'm almost thirty-one, I tell myself. I'm going to have some lines around my mouth and my eyes. Then there's the sun damage from the days of when it was cool to have a tan. I baked myself brown as almost every other teenager I knew. I would get compliments on how beautiful I looked with a tan.

Now it is fall in the Northwest and my skin is pale and shows all its faults. I've never been a big user of make-up, but I find myself reading the ads in the newspapers for facelifts, eye surgery, special bonus offers at the counters of Estee Lauder and Lanocome.

One day, I'm driving in the car, and this ad comes on the

radio. A woman is talking about how difficult it is to change careers in mid-life. The reason it is so difficult is because she has bags under her eyes and a double chin. She goes on to say that because of one-day, out-patient surgery, she gets a new face and a new job. I click off the radio in disgust. I will never go that far to make myself look young.

Destiny meets me at the front counter of the busy salon. She looks about twenty years old and she has long hair like mine. I start to relax when I see her long hair. She will know what to do to make me look beautiful.

Destiny looks part Asian and part Caucasian. She has beautiful skin and an exotic flavor to her. She is wearing a black polyester shirt with a Nehru collar and black polyester bell bottoms with little pink and yellow daisies embroidered on each pant leg. She tells me that all of the students in the beauty school have to wear black. Destiny looks like a flower child.

I sit in the swivel chair and am assaulted with a huge mirror. I do not want to look at myself for the length of the appointment in this huge reflecting mass. I try to avert my eyes, but mirrors are everywhere. Destiny fluffs my hair with her manicured hands. She asks me what I want. I'm not sure. I'm never sure when I come to these places. It's like being in another world and I feel out of place. I start to panic. I can't make a decision. I say, "Like yours would be fine."

Destiny talks me into coloring my hair. There are gray strands, and she says the color will make a big difference. "You would be amazed at the difference a color can make." I tell her that I have used a natural henna at home. She calls her supervisor over and the supervisor rakes her fingers through my hair. I feel painfully self-conscious at the scrutiny.

The supervisor advises Destiny on the coloring. I've got several tones in my hair from where I've colored it and where it's grown out. The two consult and I feel like there is something wrong with me. After the consultation, Destiny assures me that a mix of red, brown, and gold for the top portion of my hair and something called, "radiance," for the ends will do the trick. I go along with her recommendations, feeling helpless in this environment.

While Destiny mixes the color, I rip open a large manila envelope that holds a manuscript that I have been sent by a man in my writing class. There are seventy-four typed pages. I wonder that he can send me seventy-four pages when he apologized last week for not having time to read my ten-page piece that he had for over a month.

I need to distract myself from the superficiality of the salon, so I delve into the manuscript that reads like a textbook. I'm wondering who his audience will be.

Destiny comes back and brings me a cup of spiced tea in a Styrofoam cup. She tells me this is better than coffee, and I surmise that she is subtly trying to heal me of my bad habits. It is good, but I still like my coffee better.

As Destiny applies the gloppy mess of color to my hair, she talks on and on and I am unable to continue with the manuscript. She tells me about her mother's facelift. "The doctor did her eyes, too, even though she didn't ask. Now they're not healing. We're talking major lawsuit here."

Destiny tells me that we lose an average of fifty hairs a day. This fact makes a big impression on her and she repeats the figure, "Fifty hairs!" I try and read a few more lines of the manuscript and then give up. We talk about Halloween and Destiny tells me how she went to the only "real" haunted house there is when she lived in California. "Someone actually chased us with a real chain saw and you had no choice, but to run." I shake my head in amazement and she tells me, "Try and hold still. I want this to be perfect." She is brushing color through my hair with a large wide-toothed comb. The color looks like brown jello and smells of chemicals. She gets some on my forehead and I wonder if it will stain, but I don't say anything.

"Hair is art!" Destiny announces. "Doing color is my favorite." She asks me about my family and I tell her that I am thirty-one and single.

"Wow," she says. "You don't look that old. I hope that I have as much hair as you when I am older."

Destiny says," My mom is forty, but I don't know how her facelift is going to turn out yet."

Destiny leads me to a hair dryer and I sit under it with nothing to read for twenty minutes. I look around the room of practitioners of beauty all dressed in black with high heeled shoes and think that their feet must really hurt by the end of the day. Destiny later tells me that the hardest thing about her job is standing on her feet all day. Her shoes look slightly more comfortable than the others, but still have a substantial heel on them.

I've been in the salon for two hours now and I'm starting to get restless. Destiny's supervisor has suggested a "clay pack," for my hair. "This is just like a face mask, only for your hair." They have told me earlier that my hair is dry and damaged. The clay pack should do miracles. I go along with their suggestion.

Three hours later I'm sitting under the dryer, this time with manuscript in hand. All the other customers are reading fashion magazines.

At ten minutes to five, Destiny approaches me and tells me that we won't have time to do the haircut. Then she comes back a minute later and says, "My supervisor could do the haircut for you really really quick, if you'd like."

The clay has taken too long to dry and the salon is about to close. The supervisor approaches me and checks a strand of hair for dryness. "Just a few more minutes," she says. "But I'm sorry, we won't have time to do the haircut. You can schedule another appointment with Destiny."

I'm tired and saturated with hair color and clay and women in rollers. Shocks of hair are all over the floor. I really only wanted a trim. I see the "finished" women leaving and paying their bills and they look about the same as when they came in.

I tell Destiny that I will call her later for an appointment. She asks if I would be her model to work on for final exams. "You'll get a free color, you know." I am too tired to say no so I say, "Yes. That would be fine. Here's my phone number."

Finally I am released from my three hours of treatment. My hair is a little darker and a little richer. It shines and gives me a boost. I am under the illusion that I have been transformed. I give Destiny a five-dollar tip and head for the car.

In the car I brush out my hair and brown dye appears on the bristles. I can't wait to get home and wash out the chemical smell.

I look in the mirror and realize I look the same. I don't look into anymore mirrors for the rest of the night. I promise myself not to return to the salon again, but I know that promise will be broken on a rainy day when I look into the mirror and see lines and find more gray hairs framing my face.

Autobiography

WHEN YOU WERE LITTLE YOU LIKED TO SWIM. *THE WATER WAS AN embryonic net for you. You felt safe in the water. You liked to dive and float and see how long you could hold your breath, until your lungs burned and you felt that they would burst. You wondered what it would be like to take a deep breath under water. You felt that you could breathe underwater if you really wanted to. That is where you drew all your sustenance — under the musky-smelling lake water that was your home.*

Your real home was in a house on a street with a driveway and a big front door. In the summer the door stayed open and the screen door stayed shut to keep out the flies. You used to bang the screen door when you left with your towel rolled under one arm to go swim in the lake.

Inside the house, it was hard to get a deep breath of air. The air inside the house was dense and tasteless. All the good smells were outside in the electric air of summer.

Summer is the time I remember you best. Summer was penetrating sun and hot bubbling tar on the street. Summer came with a gentle force that got stronger and stronger until it was alive enough that you could feel something. The trees burst open in clouds of green. The sky was so blue it hurt your eyes to look at it. The insects, there must have been millions or trillions of them, made a constant buzzing sound like the crackling of electric wires, and you could hear those insects all day and feel the warm tar ooze between your toes and know that you were alive, that when you had been in the house all winter felt like a dream, but now you were real.

— 📖 —

When you came home from the lake, your mother would be lying on top of her king size bed, on top of the blue polyester bedspread, reading a book, and you'd go and lie with her after you ate.

The kitchen would be dark with afternoon shadows, and when you opened the refrigerator the light would leak out all over the linoleum floor and strike the cabinets. You would take out a bowel filled with summer fruit and take it to the dining room table. The dining room, it was like being inside a vault. The silence was greater than the silence inside of you inside of this house. You would pick a firm, purple plum and bite into its flesh and taste the sweetness and the sourness and suck on the pit when you were done. Then, a ripe peach and another plum. The fruit cooled your body, hot from the walk — a mile long from the lake club. The lifeguards knew you and watched you swim and disappear under the water, and you were a beautiful mermaid.

— 📖 —

The grownups never knew you. There was always this curtain between your center and the world, and it stayed closed and became heavy, like velvet covered with dust, and even if you tried to pull the cord to open this curtain and let in some light, it got stuck and wouldn't open. You stayed behind the curtain because it muffled the sounds that came shattering the house of silence that you had lived in for so long.

— 📖 —

First it was the silence, and then it was the sharp and pointed noise that cut the air like a knife. When the noise got really loud and poisoned the breathing air, you would draw the curtain closer around you, but still, it could not block out the sounds, but only muffle them and that wasn't enough.

Your body learned to take the sounds of terror and store them in your muscles. The ugly noise of voices raised against one another, fighting and fighting, one voice always weaker than the other. Your body learned to manufacture weapons and stayed vigilant all day and all night so that it could be ready to make more weapons if it needed to. Your protection was the weapon of silence.

For Me

I DECIDE TO GO TO YOGA AS A WAY TO IMPROVE MY BREATHING AND see if it can help steady my emotional life as it relates to my therapy practice. I pick yoga because I have always loved dance and movement. As a teenager, I spent many years in a semi-professional dance troupe, but I didn't like the pressure of performing.

As an adult woman I go into yoga expecting my body and mind to integrate. I do not go into it with expectations of becoming a contortionist or an ascetic living on a mountaintop. My only interest is in exploring what the big deal about breathing is all about.

The first time I come to yoga class, I wear heavy sweats and a T-shirt. Most everyone else in the class is wearing tights and sports bras. I pick a spot in the back of the room and try to go unnoticed which I soon realize is impossible. If the teacher can't hear you breathing, you're immediately noticed.

I'm physically strong so I've picked a more advanced class for my re-entry into the world of movement. We start in seated breathing (pranayama) for twenty minutes and I hear sounds as though Darth Vader was in the room. Students flush snot out of their noses and exhale in long audible "ahhhhhs." The teacher simply instructs us to notice our breathing. I am noticing everyone else's breathing without a clue to my own.

As I tune in, I notice that my breath is caught in my upper chest like a fish flopping around in a net. As my instructor encourages me to deepen my breath, I get confused. Deepen? Where? How? I thought this was supposed to be simple.

Sunlight warms the yoga studio's wooden floors. I try to connect to my breath again. It comes through the corridor of my being in spurts like water through a garden hose that has lain dormant through the winter season and is now turned on for the first time.

I feel my diaghram constrict around the air flow hampering its free passage. I am aware of the muscle tension that clamps down on free and spontaneous movement. If I let this go, what would happen? I use muscles to support me more than my skeleton. I don't trust my bones. I don't know them like I know the familiar grabbing of my muscles.

My teacher's voice sings out to me sometimes in English, sometimes in Sanskrit.

This is a place where my heart can break completely open and spill its contents all over the floor, and still I will emerge whole.

The simplicity of breath and movement that makes yoga, or union of mind, body, and spirit, tells me that we are nothing more than who and what we are.

PART IV

BUILDING UP

"It is easier to pull down than to build up."
–Latin Proverb

The Kids

H E DRAWS MY HEART OUTSIDE MY BODY IN THE UPPER LEFTHAND corner of the page, like a return address. He concentrates grinding the black crayon around and around giving the heart a thick rind.

While Julian is doing this, my brother burns down the old New England Church on Third and Main.

I'm supposed to fix this child. Julian is five years old. We're getting to the end of our sessions and still he draws himself and a salmon and they look the same — amorphous orange shapes divided with a horizontal line.

I have told Julian that it is our second to last time together. Is that why he is drawing a picture of me with my heart plucked out of my body? After he finishes his drawing, Julian wraps himself in a plastic tablecloth. I rub my palm up and down his spine listening to the rasping sound of my skin against vinyl.

I am seven. I am riding my bicycle past the church that my brother burns down thirty years later. As a young girl, I never noticed the church. I was more interested in the wedge of graveyard across the street. Some of the headstones read "girl" or "boy" and were dated into the early 1800s. The children in these graves only lasted three or four days on earth.

— 📖 —

Sally is leaving. Ten years old. Changing schools again. Sally with the cussing mouth. Sally in overalls that hang off her collarbone and come halfway up her calves. Sally with the scraggly hair that looks like it has never been brushed, but is always clean. Sally, the girl who loves animals and steals jewel studded pet collars and other cat paraphernalia from K-Mart. She steals nothing for herself, but is the first to be accused when something is missing from the classroom.

The church is burning, erupting in flames and a victim is pulled out — my brother. He is wearing Adidas running shoes and a gray sweatshirt over jeans. He behaves more like a drowning man than one dying in a fire. He hooks his rescuers around the neck and tries to run back into the church. The voices my brother was hearing had ordered him to die. That is why he has set the fire. No one will let him die.

Alex reflexively twists her fingers around her non-existent curls. Finding only brown stubble on her scalp now, she lets her head drop and fidgets with her skirt. Alex is six. She is shy when she sees me again after two years. I knew her when she was four and her head overflowed with golden corkscrew curls. Her parents shaved her head to get rid of the lice.

After the ashes of the church have been blasted with tens of thousands of gallons of water, the people come alone and in small groupings. With shovels and hoes, they fill buckets with debris and cart away wheelbarrows full of destruction. They dump the charred planks and water-soaked pieces of wall and roof and transom and beams into a pile along the road. All day long and into the night, the wheelbarrows move like a funeral procession. "Who could have done such a thing?" they think.

My father pushes a wheelbarrow. It is drizzling outside. His arms are stiff from the effort of plunging his garden shovel into layers of muck. The smell of smoke is still strong and its sharpness cuts into the back of his throat and offends his lungs. He leans on his shovel for a moment and stares at the place where the church used to be. His son is safe and warm and heavily sedated. His son cannot feel.

Candace likes to flirt with me. She jumps into my lap whenever I am sitting down and if I am standing she knocks me off balance with her enormous hugs. Candace covers her ears with her hands when her Kindergarten room gets too noisy. Candace comes to school dressed in hot pink matching sweatsuits with bright bows and braids in her hair. Candace wants a new mom. Any kind, adult female will do. Candace punches her classmates with her fist when they have something that she wants. She wets her bed at night and sometimes wets her pants at school. Candace loves to play house, and that is what she would do all day if she had the chance. Candace tells me that she has seven imaginary friends. I ask her who her real friends in the classroom are. I ask her to point to them, but she tells me, "I already told you. These are my friends," and gestures upward into space.

Vali is eleven. He tells me that his mother is dead. He says, "dead," like it is the last word in the English language. Vali tells me that his mother was strong when she was alive, before the cancer. He picks up the stapler on my desk and tries to break it in two.

I can't tell you the exact moment that my oldest brother began to become capable of burning down a church. The kid who was terrified of germs. The boy who had no friends. The brilliant child who refused to shine. My brother stands stiffly in shorts and a white shirt, not even an attempt of a smile for the camera. All of the pictures are in black and white. I can't know when or how he became so sick.

I remember laughing at his made-up songs with characters that were Dr. Seuss-like: "Ash Crow and the Osprey-oops." I remember loving this brother for his sweet nature and kindness. When he start stalking me and exposing himself to me as a young girl and became a predator, I became shut down. He kept me a prisoner in my own home.

My youngest brother is quick and bright and breaks his leg in a skiing accident when he is four. He is fearless and recovers perfectly. When he is seven, he and his friend tear off the heads of my dolls: the dolls I had collected for years, from places my grandmother had been; Tahiti, Kenya, England. The heads and limbs have been ripped off my dolls and thrown into a pile where the body parts are mixed up and exchanged so that arms and legs stick out from the wrong orifices of broken dolls. But this brother does not get sick in the way that my oldest brother does. None of us do in this way.

Sally talks to me of the five-bedroom house that she will move into. She will have twenty cats and three dogs. She models animals out of clay and draws with white chalk on black construction paper, pictures of cats. When Sally dreams about her new house she is far away. Her eyes are focused beyond me and out my office window, somewhere that I have never been. I don't go with her. I wait for her at the table until she returns.

I have been at this elementary school for a month. It is famous for its proportion of high-risk children; I am the resident counselor. I am married now, to the cornerstone of my personal support, and know the joy of ushering new life.

I am the only girl. I am the second youngest, one of the middle children. I wear gold stretch pants with a matching gold and blue-striped shirt. My other outfit is purple stretch pants with a matching purple and red shirt. My teeth are in braces. When I pose for photographs in my black velvet dress, I smile with my mouth closed, to hide the braces. I am in fourth grade, Sally's age, and I perch on the end of a marble coffee table for the picture after Sunday School. Like Sally, I steal things, but not for pets or for myself. I steal things from people. It's not that I want or need the things. It's to see if anyone notices.

When I am a younger girl, maybe eight years old, I tell my mother one day that, "All music makes me sad." The radio is playing a jaunty tune. I insist that it makes me sad to hear this music, and my mother is confused. She asks me why. I say, "I don't know," and she wipes her hands on her apron and continues to polish the buffet with Lemon Pledge. I like the smell of the lemon, but I don't tell her that.

I am away at college when my brother is first hospitalized. He is involuntarily committed to a private mental hospital before he ever has regular visits with a psychiatrist on an outpatient basis. His disease is chronic and progressive. They can find nothing physically wrong with him. His diagnosis is imprecise: "Schizophrenic, Manic Depressive, Obsessive-Compulsive," and has our whole family on edge. We don't know what has happened, what is happening, and what could happen in the future.

After burning down the church, my brother is in jail on arson charges. He is under psychiatric supervision. He is on a suicide watch.

He calls me and says, "This is the best place I've ever been. The food is better than any mental hospital and the guards play basketball with me."

Soon he is transferred to a state mental hospital. His phone calls are less frequent and when he does call, his words are thickened by the effect of the powerful neuroleptic medication, Haldol. My brother spends much of his time inside state mental institutions. The money for private-pay has run out.

I want to be a healer of children because I am desperate to find out where it all begins. I must know. It will all come out if I work long and hard enough. The children talk to me. I fall in love with them. I work best when I am in love.

Sally

SALLY: JUTTING COLLAR BONES, DEEP AND THROATY VOICE, TEN years old. When she smiles, her whole face moves and comes alive. It lasts for barely a second. Then, the smile is quickly swallowed up by some part of her that is eager to eat the smile and store it somewhere deep inside of her to be saved for later.

Freckles spray across the bridge of Sally's nose. Her eyes are luminous feline green. Sally. So bravado, so scared. "My brother, Chet, lets me in his room. He gives me a drag off his cigarette. He sleeps in the garage, and I get to go in. He won't let Mitch in. He's a brat."

Sally gets suspended from school now and then, mostly for stealing. She tells me she is falsely accused of stealing at school. Whenever anything is missing from the classroom, Sally is scapegoated. She tells me that she only steals things from the pet department at the K-Mart. Her brother Chet is fifteen and he steals cigarettes. Mitch is six and he steals candy.

Sally looks unhealthy to me. The school nurse agrees, but we tread lightly. The last school that Sally attended called her mother and said that her daughter was underweight and had failed the hearing test in her right ear. Sally's mom pulled her out of school. She never got to finish second grade.

Sally is now in the fourth grade. Her attendance has been regular, although she is late to school by at least twenty minutes every day. She comes to see me every Tuesday at ten o'clock and we talk for half an hour or forty-five minutes. She arrives right on time for her counseling appointment.

Every week, Sally tells me that she is tired, and then she tells me that she is hungry. But when I give her a piece of fruit or half of my sandwich for lunch, she says, "Thanks," nibbles at the food absentmindedly and never finishes it. One time I gave her a chocolate bar and she took a little bite and saved the rest.

Sally doesn't show much interest in "kid" things. She spends most of her time hanging out with her older brother and her mother and her mother's friends. She talks about partying, and she talks about cats. These are the two things that interest her.

Sally often comes to her counseling sessions with several books on cats that she has checked out from the library. One book that Sally really loves is a large, thick picture book, *All About Cats.* She likes to sit with me and show me her favorite pictures. When she gets to the section with the Persian and other exotic and expensive cats, Sally strokes the animals on the page with her fingertips.

When Sally gets to the section on diseases of cats, she likes to read the caption that goes with the disfigured and sick cats. She has fun "grossing me out," as she goes on to read the paragraphs that go with the pictures. She can always count on a reaction from me. My gross-out reaction makes Sally laugh. She says, "What?" Like: What's the matter with you? Sally likes it that I can't stand to look at these pictures without flinching, yet she can.

The books are almost always overdue. The librarian is sympathetic up to a point, but when Sally's family moves away again, they owe more than forty dollars in fines for lost and unreturned books and the librarian is not quite so forgiving.

Sally's records cannot be transferred to the new school until the library fines are paid. The fines are not paid and Sally's new teachers struggle to understand this child from scratch. In some ways, I think this is a good thing, for the teachers not to get the records ahead of time and hold on to some preconceived notion of what this child is about. On the other hand, I get several calls from the counselor at the new school desperate for information that will help her and Sally's teachers understand her.

Sally treats me with respect. She addresses me as "Mrs. W." and says please and thank you when she wants something or when I give her something. But in the hallway, her teacher often stops me and tells me what a problem Sally is. "The whole class got held in from recess again because Sally refused to admit she had stolen the three quarters in the top of my desk drawer. She's impossible. I know her home life is terrible, but I'm going nuts."

I listen to Sally's teacher and think of the girl who brings me small clay figurines of cats that she has modeled and stuck inside a clear box. I think of the girl who wipes her nose on her sleeve and asks me how to spell poetry when I tell her what I like to read.

The first time we meet, Sally lets me ask her questions like, "What is your favorite food? How many brothers and sisters do you have? What is your favorite T.V. show?"

She tells me her favorite T.V. show is *Beavis and Butthead.*

At first, Sally doesn't want to know anything about me. She doesn't want to look at any of my toys. She sits at the table and squishes this mushy pumpkin head I have on the table, into silly shapes.

"I can kill this thing," she says. After Sally puts the pumpkin down, she decides to ask me a few things, like, "How old are you? Are you married? How old are your kids? What's your favorite T.V. show?" I can't think of one. I tell her that I like to read, but I can't think of a favorite book. Sally asks, "Did you ever steal anything?"

"Well, I think I might have stolen something at about the time I was in fourth grade. I stole my brother's baseball cards and I felt really sick inside about it," I tell her.

I remember telling my first major lie about stealing the cards. I took a shoebox full of them and hid them at my next door neighbor's house. My friend Lori and I shoved them underneath her bed. We didn't even open the box to look at the cards. At the time, I didn't know what the motivation for stealing was. Now I know that it was to see if I could get away with it.

My father lined up my three brothers and some stray neighbor kids who happened to be walking by. He demanded to know who took the cards. It was a hot summer day, but I shivered in my shorts and T-shirt.

I started to lie about the cards. I made up a story about who might have done it and why. "It must have been a boy who didn't have any of their own cards. Only a boy would be interested in baseball cards." Then I started to wither like a wad of paper thrown into a raging fire.

My father was relentless in his cross-examination. I broke down and confessed. I don't remember what my punishment was or if that was it, just standing in that line of kids, knowing that my dad knew that I was the one.

"I steal," Sally announces looking right at me. "My mother doesn't buy nothin' but food."

"What do you like to steal?"

"Stuff from the pet department. Little toys for cats. I love cats. Once Mitchell stole candy from the video store and my mother grabbed him real hard by the arm, like this," she said, digging her fingers into my bicep, "and marched him back into the store and made him tell the lady. He never stole again. I never get caught."

I observe this skinny girl in front of me. At our first meeting, she lifted up her T-shirt to reveal a long raised scar that cleaved her chest in two. She told me that the scar was made soon after she was born, because of a heart problem. "They had to patch up these three holes in my heart."

I look at the unkempt child gnawing on the apple I have brought for her. She chews off the skin and spits the peelings into the garbage can. I think of how logical it is for her to steal.

I'm afraid that she'll get caught, though. "You know, Sally, if you got caught stealing, it would be a really nasty scene. Maybe there are some other ways you could get the things that you need. Do you get an allowance?"

"No."

Our conversation is at a standstill. I know that things are not the real deficit. She doesn't want all the chocolate that I have to offer her. She takes just one little piece and nibbles a corner off of it and stuffs the rest into her pants pocket.

I write on a piece of paper. "I like Sally. I look forward to seeing you each week."

Sally writes, "I like Mrs. W. She treats me nice."

— 📖 —

After a few weeks of seeing me for counseling, Sally started to come down to my office at all times of the day for any excuse. She thought she might have left her notebook in my office. She was sure her overdue library book was under the stack of papers on my desk. She needed to tell me that she would be five minutes late for our next appointment.

One day Sally came to my office door and it was closed because I was seeing another student. I saw Sally's face pressed up against the rectangular glass window in my door and her look of shock that turned into sadness when she saw I was playing pick-up sticks with another girl her age. Pick-up sticks was one of Sally's favorite games and we were used to playing it over and over again while we talked about the dreams and disappointments of her life. By the time I got up from my chair to acknowledge Sally, she was gone. I tried to find her later, but she was taking an achievement test in class and could not be disturbed.

The next week we met, I asked Sally how she had felt seeing me with another child. She shrugged and said, "I don't care," in her nasal tone. Sally always seemed to be fighting off a cold.

"I care." I said and waited. We sat in silence.

"I care tremendously for you Sally."

Sally's head was bent over some pieces of cloth she had brought with her to our session. Her fingers twisted up the cloth and smoothed it and twisted it up again around her index finger.

After a few moments Sally said, "I told my mom that I wanted chocolate cake for my birthday and she made a carrot cake with little orange frosting carrots on top. It was so dumb."

I wanted to do things for Sally.

I got her a new coat from the donations that came to school, but not just any old coat. I pulled three of the best ones in her size and let her pick which one she wanted. She picked the black, fake leather jacket. It looked good on her. It emphasized her toughness.

I liked that Sally could be so tough and so feminine at the same time. She wasn't that in touch with her feminine side, but one time she let me brush her hair for the class pictures. She looked really beautiful with her hair combed out, the sharp angles of her face more prominent.

About two weeks before Sally's birthday, she sent me notes in my faculty mailbox and reminded me every time that she saw me in the hallway that her birthday was coming.

The secretary got mad at Sally one day for coming into the office without asking. She was trying to sneak a note into my box. The secretary told me, " I can't have a girl like this back here. We handle money and all kinds of things. You know she steals."

I said, "She won't bother you again."

I caught Sally in the hall later in the day and pulled her aside. "You know Sally, Mrs. K. gets a little uptight sometimes. I heard you had a run in with her in the office today. Try to let it go. It's not your fault."

That was the first time I saw Sally cry. "I didn't do anything to her. She hates me." Sally was inconsolable, and I invited her down to my office. I held her while she cried and wrote her an excuse note so she wouldn't get in trouble when she went back to class.

On her birthday Sally brought in a dozen chocolate cupcakes that she had made by herself from a mix at home. She spent the session deciding who to give the precious cupcakes to. There were only twelve cupcakes and there were so many teachers and schoolmates that she wanted to give one to. She wrote a little card to go with each one. The one for Mrs. K. read, "Enjoy. It's my birthday. Love, Sally."

Around the time of winter break, Sally started to bring me little presents every time she came down to see me. The first was a braided friendship bracelet. She was trying to sell the bracelets for fifty cents a piece to the secretaries and teachers, and other kids in the school, and people were actually buying these things even though it was against school policy to promote private enterprise.

Then it was clay. Sally would bring me funny little shapes fashioned out of clay and Playdough.

One day she brought a clear, Lucite box full of blue clay pieces and a note stuck in. "I love you, Mrs. W." I still have this box on my desk and try to think of Sally now as strong and successful out there in the world.

Sally told me one day after the winter break, that her family would be moving at the end of the month, the end of February, just three weeks away. I could see that Sally was unsettled. She wouldn't look at me. She twisted her hair around her index finger. It looked like her hair hadn't been washed since the last time I had seen her two weeks ago. She had lost weight. Her overalls hung on her body like they were stretched over a rack.

The house they were to move into was huge, Sally told me. "Five bedrooms. I get my own room. And it's on five acres. We're going to get a whole bunch of cats and some dogs, too … my mom said."

For three more weeks it was the fantasy of the house and the acreage. Nothing more. No people, friends, or grandmothers in the picture.

I was having trouble visualizing this house as anything but large and empty. I think underneath it all Sally was most afraid of the emptiness, too. But when it came time to say goodbye, she pulled out of her slump and seemed to be genuinely happy about the move.

The goodbye was hard for me. Sally gave me a quick hug and a smile and was out the door. My eyes teared up as I watched her lope down the hallway in the denim overalls that I was used to seeing her in.

I kept thinking about Sally; how hard it would be for her to adjust to a new school and make new friends and just plain make it, day to day. Her dream of the house kept my hope alive. What formerly had been a phantom, now was real. The house had to be there as she was promised it would be. I embroidered it with the warmth of a fireplace, family dinners with heaping dishes of steaming food, fresh linen on the beds that had been hung to dry in the morning sun and still held the smell of fresh air.

When the counselor at the new school called, I was excited like a child. I couldn't wait to call back and hear all about Sally. But when I called the counselor back I had a sinking feeling. Why would she be calling? Certainly not to report good news.

The counselor sounded perky. "Sally has been coming to school, but late most days." I felt reassured if that was her only concern, but then the counselor's voice became softer and more emphatic like she was telling me secrets. "You know, she refuses to do any work. She says it's too hard and then cries. Especially with math. Do you know at what grade level she tested out in, in math?"

I knew things were bad for Sally and I hated it that the counselor was focusing on her schoolwork. My mind went fuzzy while the counselor talked on. "We weren't able to obtain her school record because of the hold until all the overdue library fees were paid. Do you know how long that may take, for mom to pay the forty-three dollar fine? These records would really help us out." I wanted to hang up, but first I wanted to implore this woman to see: *Please see this girl.*

Instead, I asked about the house. I was told that there never was a house or land or cats and dogs.

Sally's family had been living in a rusted-out old trailer with no plumbing and a leaky roof. Public Health was called out on a home visit after Sally and her three brothers arrived at school dirty, hungry, and their hair full of lice. The trailer had been condemned and the family needed to find new housing in a week's time. "We really don't have any public housing out here," the counselor whined. "Perhaps a move back into your area would be the appropriate thing to do."

My brother had to be over forty. I had lost track of the years. I knew he was at least four years older than me. He had grown bloated from medications. He lived as a groundskeeper on an estate in suburbia. He hung onto shreds of sanity as long as he could and then lost it — lost his tether to this earth.

Ellie

ELLIE IS THE KEEPER OF THE DOLLHOUSE. SHE RUNS THE PLAY-room dollhouse like a caretaker in an orphanage for babies and lost dogs.

Ellie was neglected from infancy. Her birth parents used heroin and couldn't take care of her; she was weaned off of heroin with morphine and other drugs during her first five days of life. Two of her siblings had already been placed in foster homes by the State. At age one, a loving family adopted her.

It is very important to Ellie that the doll babies get fed almost continuously. She makes them huge meals of colored stones and serves them up on tiny plates. I have had to add eight babies since Ellie started coming to see me.

Ellie is four with light brown skin and kinky black hair that twirls down her back. Whenever she comes into the playroom she goes right to the dollhouse and makes sure the babies are okay — all eleven of them. There are three dogs, too. She makes sure that all of the adult dolls are locked up in toy bins. "They can't come out," she says, "because they used drugs and now they are in heaven." Her birth parents are actually alive, but are denied visitation.

One day Ellie inspected the dollhouse and found one of the dogs missing. She enlisted my help in searching for the dog. It was a hard session for Ellie, with eleven babies to feed and a lost dog to find. We searched in every desk drawer, file cabinet and toy box and shelf and could not find the lost dog. We looked under all the cushions and mattresses in the two-story dollhouse and could not find the missing dog. Ellie was distraught. I couldn't let a kid with her history leave the session worried about a lost dog that she was so attached to.

I asked Ellie if she had any ideas of how we might find the lost dog. She shrugged her shoulders. "I wonder what we could do?" I asked. She was at a loss. I was tapping my fingers on a stack of yellow sticky pads on my desk. Ellie would often take a few sheets of sticky notes with her when she left to hold her over until the next session.

"Hey Ellie," I said, "I've got an idea. How about if we put up some notices around the office — you know signs — 'Has anyone seen a lost dog?'"

Ellie brightened up and started to peel sticky notes off the pad and place them on my desk. She handed me a pen and said, "Write." I wrote: Lost Dog. Please call Ellie or Martha at 555-5252. I wrote this ten times on little yellow squares and Ellie leaped around the office sticking the squares on the dollhouse, the couch, the lamp, and out in the waiting area — on the coffeepot, *Newsweek* magazine, and any place she could find where she thought people might see the signs.

The next day, I went to the toy store where I had bought the miniature cocker spaniel and they were all out. They didn't know where I might find another one just like it. I drove all over town looking at plastic replicas of all breeds of dogs, but couldn't find the exact one that was missing from Ellie's orphanage.

I never did find the exact replacement for the dog, but I got something close and when Ellie saw it the next week, she said, "Look, his brother has come home." Considering she had never seen her own brother, but knew he existed, I felt this was progress. This is still her favorite dog, and she makes sure that he is tucked into the crib with the tiniest baby before she leaves session for the week.

Candace

MOST KIDS, HOWEVER MISTREATED, WANT TO PROTECT THEIR parents. They are attached to their parents. The attachment may be thin and worn in places, or it may be fused with scar tissue, but for young children, their primary caretakers are their world. Abused children consider abuse to be normal. It is all they know. If they disclose, they feel guilty and often recant. Guilt and shame run like two deep veins down the spine of an abused child.

Six-year-old Candace Grant was different. She openly detested both of her parents. When she talked about her parents, she would gesture wildly with her arms to illustrate how chaotic her family life was. Unlike other kids, she did not appear to swallow the blame for her parents' bad behavior. She just wanted out — anywhere — just out from the trailer camp she lived in with her dad and her sister.

When I first met Candace, she looked me in the eye and asked, "Can I go with you?" Her eyes held steady as she waited for my answer. She dropped the scissors she was using to cut around the outline of her green dinosaur painting.

"Today we'll visit in your classroom," I said. "Another day, you can come to my office."

"I don't want to go to your office. I want to go home with you." Candace coldcocked me with her words. We had just met and yet as I was to find out, Candace was supremely sure of herself. I squirmed under her dark gaze. She waited. She waited some more. Then she said, "Well?" She was standing now with her hands on her hips.

I considered taking this child home. It seemed like a simple thing to do.

"I can't take you home with me, Candace, it's against the rules."

"Sourbones," she said, and skulked away whispering obscenities under her breath.

— 📖 —

I had visited Candace in her classroom after her father had come to see me.

Mr. Grant wore tight jeans with a silver chain hooked from his belt loop to his pocket. A tank top covered a pot belly and showed off tattoos all up and down his arms. It looked like he hadn't shaved in days, and when I ushered him into my office I noticed a strong smell of marijuana.

"Thank you for coming in Mr. Grant," I said, extending my hand. "Jake. You can call me Jake," he said. He took a seat in my desk chair and I sat across the table from him in a child's plastic chair.

Jake told me that Candy had been raped by his former girlfriend's son when she was three. "She still talks about it, to strangers in the elevator. It's embarrassing the way she uses the correct terms and all for the body parts."

Later in our conversation, he brought the rape up again using slang words for body parts — watching for a reaction from me.

I felt, at times, that Jake was lying. It was such a hard-luck story. I believed some of it: the kids' mother — mentally ill, hospitalized for suicidal depression. She had a history as an abusive parent. Because of all the mess with the mother, Jake had been awarded full custody of both children, but they still visited their mother every other weekend.

Jake talked about his ex-wife's boyfriend, Bill. There was the time Bill put a gun to his mouth in front of his daughters, Anabel and Candy and called their mother at the bar where she was working. "Kathy, you get your ass home this minute, or I'll blow my head off in front of your kids."

Jake pumped his foot and leg some more. He made me nervous. I could feel this pent up energy in him that could explode at any moment. Everything about Jake was held. Aside from the jangly leg, the rest of him was still. Too still.

Jake's brow was furrowed. Small trenches of line had formed around his mouth and eyes. His skin had a gray pallor to it. The tattoo on his right bicep was of a barebreasted woman entwined around a rope.

Jake didn't want to report any of the things he had told me to the authorities or stop visitation of his children to his ex-wife's apartment. I thought this was odd, especially given the gun incident. These things have to be reported. Was child welfare not on top of this?

Jake pointed his finger at me and said, "I want you to be my kid's counselor." I told him I would refer him to a community agency. He said, "I don't have any money."

After I refused him, Jake became conciliatory. "I'm desperate. I don't know what else to do, but to come and see you." He buried his head in his hands and I couldn't tell if he was crying or not.

I wanted to help this man and his kids and I felt manipulated by him. I felt threatened when he pointed his finger at me, raised his voice, and then told me about his gun collection. I wanted him to leave. I looked at my watch and saw that we had been talking for close to an hour. Still, I let him stay a while longer.

Jake must have sensed my impatience because he got real for one moment. He stopped tapping his foot up and down. He leaned forward in my desk chair and positioned his elbows on his thighs. He told me that he loved his job as a collections agent. He was excellent at harassing people until they broke. He made seven dollars and fifty cents an hour at this job. He refused to go on welfare and he refused to give up his kids.

"I guess I just like being a jerk." Jake looked down when he said this, but when he was finished, he flashed me with a shy grin and there were tears in his eyes.

After Mr. Grant left, I went to visit Candace in her classroom. She was sitting on the floor cutting around the border of a giant green dinosaur she had painted in poster paint. She had her hair all done in bows and braids with a slick of black bangs falling below her eyebrows. Jake had told me that he could "braid hair and keep food in the cabinets."

I knew right away that I didn't want to do therapy with Candace. I wanted to hold her. I wanted to be this girl's mother.

When the bell rang for recess, Candy ignored it and kept on talking to me. She didn't know that I was a counselor, but she talked to me as if she knew. She told me about Bill and the back rubs and beatings and the gun to the mouth story and I wrote notes on the trimmings of her dinosaur picture in a fat red pencil.

Jake had told me that "Candy tells some mighty good stories," but everything she said matched his stories about the rape at three, the gun, etc. So, they were both lying or both telling the truth about these things.

Candy moved closer to me until she was sitting on my lap. We talked about her mom and dad and Mom's boyfriend, Bill, and Dad's girlfriend, Abby.

I thanked Candace for talking. I said, goodbye and told her that I would come to see her again. I had my hand on the door-knob and Candace was pulling at my skirt. She pleaded with me, "Take me too ... please." I told her I'd see her again tomorrow.

Referral

IBELIEVED JAKE DID LOVE HIS CHILDREN, AND THERE WAS A BOND. But he certainly wasn't doing anything to protect them from obvious dangers. The situation had to be monitored, but it was more than I could do.

The referral to Child Protective Services went like this:

Child's name, birth date, siblings?
Parent's name, address, phone.
Your name, position, address.
Do you wish to be anonymous?
Reason for referral.

I wanted to tell the intake worker everything, but I knew the system only too well: what would and would not hold enough weight to constitute an investigation. The fact that Candace had a history of sex abuse and was forced to give Bill backrubs, alone were not enough. The story about the gun happened six months ago and was based on a six year old's words only. Her father would not call to corroborate the story. At the end of my long and complicated report, the intake worker said, "And what makes you think that getting beaten with a belt warrants an investigation? Have you seen any marks on the children?"

"Have you seen any marks on the children?" The absurdity of the question infuriated me, but I knew the law. Without physical evidence, tangible, measurable, scientific data, nothing would be done.

I felt hopeless. I became enraged. I started to argue with the guy on the other end of the phone. "What does it take? A child to be half dead before you'll look at this? You don't think that a child who throws tantrums before visitation, cries, and digs her heels in and has to be physically carried to her mother's place is not demonstrating reason enough to check things out? A child who in meeting me in the first thirty seconds asks that I take her home with me. A child who was raped at three and now is forced to give backrubs to a grown man ... the belt beatings...?" My voice trailed off. I knew that I was being irrational; that nothing I said would change the status of my report from "informational only" to "twenty-four hour emergency."

I told the intake worker that the kids were there now, visiting this mentally ill mother and abusive boyfriend who liked to taunt the kids: "Should we tie up Candy now? Or maybe we should just mess with Anabel tonight."

— 📖 —

When you get involved with the system, be prepared to die. The system for protecting children is inexact, imperfect, and in the end, everyone becomes a victim.

The system is a huge monster with multiple heads. The information that you have documented must be scientifically proven. If a child says they have been beaten, they have to show welts or bruises where the beating occurred. They have to say if the beating was with their clothes on or off. They have to say when the beating occurred, for how long, and with what instrument they were beaten. They have to say if this happened one time or happened many other times. Often children have to remove their clothing in front of a complete stranger and show them their body: front, back and sideways.

When a child is interviewed by a caseworker from the system, they have to be able to demonstrate to the worker that they know the difference between a truth and a lie. They have to demonstrate that they are oriented in all three spheres: person, time, and place. That is, they have to show that they are not delusional, or paranoid, or have any other kind of thought disorder. They must be able to state their full name, the time of day or what year it is (depending on their age) and where they live.

When a child is interviewed by a caseworker from the system, they must be careful not to contradict themselves. Everything they say will be scrutinized. The caseworker will snap open his or her briefcase and take out a thick pad of regulation, lined paper. Done with their interview, the caseworker will say, "Thank you," and leave.

When the caseworker leaves, the child will wonder what just happened. They will feel like they have been dreaming, but slowly they will wake up to blue plastic chairs and a small round table with clay on it and know that they are in the counselor's office.

The child might ask the counselor if they are in trouble. They may wonder, but not ask if their parents are in trouble. Almost always, they will believe that they have caused trouble, irrevocable trouble. The kind of trouble that will not go away.

— 📖 —

As soon as she spotted me, Candace ran from the group circle time and jumped into my arms nearly knocking me over. I asked if we could talk a little and she nodded her head ferociously.

Candy told me that Anabel had gotten in trouble with her dad's girlfriend, Abby, and had to stay at home. Candy demonstrated the way that Annie had scratched herself raking her fingers over and over her face. I asked her what had happened.

"Well, I can't say the word," and she pointed to her chest. "Annie grabbed these."

I said, "Anabel grabbed at Abby's breasts?" and Candace nodded and giggled.

"Then what happened?"

"She got mad and put her in her room."

"But what about the scratches?"

"Annie did it to herself."

I went back to my office. There was a phone message from Jake. He told me about the fight between Anabel and Abby. Like before, his story matched his daughter's. Jake told me that Annie had "scratched the tar out of her own face and beat her head against the floor until it was all bruised up." He told me that Anabel had also bruised Abby in five places.

Jake appealed to me for help again. I put him off. I told him I'd call some mental health agencies and get him in for a free or reduced fee. I wanted to get Jake off the phone so I could call Child Protective Services. I had to believe that this time, they would do something. The system was my only hope.

＊ 📖 ＊

I was afraid for Annie at home alone with the woman she had tangled with. I was afraid of what Abby had told the nurse on the third day that Annie didn't come to school; that she had a double ear infection and something wrong with her arm that required X-rays. Her face was also "all messed up, but she done it to herself."

I knew that I had to protect the kids, but I felt that I was betraying this family at the same time. I was afraid that the system would eat them up. They would never receive the help that they really needed. I tried to think of another way to handle this, but there was none. I was a legally mandated reporter. I made the call.

This time, I got a different intake worker and she spent half an hour getting down all the details that had roots as old as the children. She put the case on twenty-four hour emergency. The next morning, I met the investigative caseworker in the front office.

Sheila Walker extended her hand, and we gripped each other firmly in a handshake. She had dark hair and tanned skin and kind of looked like me, except for the sunglasses on top of her head pushing her hair back from her face.

We started in on the case, talking comfortably in my office. Sheila refused coffee, intent on her work. She asked me how I liked being a school counselor and I said, "Good, except that it gets lonely."

After a few minutes, Candy's teacher tapped on the door. She came in holding a white piece of construction paper. Her face was drawn. She was trying to help us in our investigation. She read off of the paper, "Candace has been extremely aggressive today." "Extremely," had been underlined twice. Then the teacher folded the paper carefully in half and looked at us. She sounded apologetic. "Really, I had to separate her from the other children. She's been hitting kids."

Sheila and I got back to work. We sat around the small kids table in little plastic chairs. It felt good to tell someone everything I knew about this family. I started talking faster and tried to slow down when I could see that Sheila was having trouble keeping up with me and writing all this stuff down. Pretty soon, Candace came in and jumped into my lap and threw her arms around my neck.

I introduced her to Sheila. Sheila talked to Candace for a long time, telling her what her job was: "to keep children safe." Then she amended her statement, "I *try* and keep children safe." I knew how often kids told of what was going on at home and it wasn't enough for an intervention — they ended up getting punished for telling.

Sheila said, "All day long, I talk to kids about what makes them happy or sad or mad, and I write it all down. All day, I write and write. It seems like all I do is write down stuff kids say all day." Candace giggled and went over to Sheila to look at her pad of lined paper. Then she returned to me and sat on my lap and gave me a big squeeze hug.

Candace was delighted with the attention of two doting women. She was wearing a hot pink sweatsuit with a pink bow in her hair. Someone obviously cared enough about her to fix her hair and keep her clothes clean. I offered her a chair and she started to play with a clay tea set another child had made. I put out some new modeling clay and she got really excited.

We each took a piece of clay and worked it while we talked. I could see that Sheila was doing a good job of interviewing by the way she kept Candace engaged and focused and was getting a lot of response to her questions, so I tried to stay out of it, only interjecting a question once in awhile.

The hardest thing about interviewing children is not to ask leading questions. I could tell when Sheila was getting close to something important and was about to ask a leading question because she would stall for a second and take another tack.

Halfway through the interview, I got tired. I thought that Sheila was taking too long. She was framing all of her questions around suspicions of sex abuse by the mother's boyfriend, Bill, but I believed Candace when she said, "All I ever did was give back rubs and I don't give him back rubs anymore.

I was more concerned about why Anabel was absent from school. I was concerned about the physical and emotional abuse that was occurring in both the mother and the father's home. But Sheila kept asking about the back rubs and Candace finally shouted, "I told you. I don't do that anymore."

I went to get a granola bar and some candy for Candace. Candace ate up her granola bar leaving crumbs on her chair and sat in my lap eating all of the chocolate kisses that I had intended for all of us to share.

Sheila kept firing off questions, and Candy started to answer by whispering into my ear and then pointing to Sheila saying, "Tell her." We proceeded this way for about twenty minutes with Candy whispering into my ear and me saying to Sheila, "Candy wants me to tell you that everyone in her house is grouchy, grumpy, and crunchy. She says to tell you that sometimes she gets beaten so hard that she sees ghosts."

The interview lasted over an hour, and we were all exhausted at the end. Sheila excused Candace, but not before Candy instructed her to write, "I love you Candace" on a piece of paper and give it to her.

I walked Candy to her after-school daycare, and the cops arrived to escort Sheila to the trailer park where she would finish her investigation by interviewing Jake and his girlfriend.

Sheila called me the next day and told me how Jake had cried "real tears." He broke down and confessed to using drugs and hitting the kids in the face. He begged her not to take his children away, and Sheila had said, "If I was going to do that, I wouldn't have sent the officer away and we'd be having this conversation downtown in my office."

Sheila set up a contract with Jake for drug treatment, family counseling, and put a stop to visitation to the mother's residence pending further investigation. She put in place some other services that were designed to keep the family together under The Family Preservation Act of Washington.

I visited Candace on the playground the next day. She straddled me on my lap and pleaded with me to take her home for the weekend. We played for awhile on the asphalt. She addressed me as "Mom," and kept asking me for permission to do things: "Is it all right if I go get some dog food at the store?" "It's okay," I said, "but be back in five minutes." Each time she would ask for permission, leave and then come back to give me a hug.

At the end of recess I walked her to her classroom and she asked me for my phone number. I said I couldn't give her my home phone number, but I could write down the school's number. I wrote the number down for her on a piece of paper toweling and told her that I wouldn't be at school during the weekend. She begged me again to take her home and clung to me until I had to pry her off of my body and say goodbye.

The contract that Sheila set up for Jake Grant was mostly a piece of paper with very little power. Nothing in the contract was court-ordered. Everything in the contract was "strongly recommended," so when Jake came in to school one day and told me that his U.A.'s (urinary analyses) had been clean, well, actually two had been a "little dirty," I wasn't surprised.

Jake had admitted to using drugs and getting a little heavy handed with his kids at times. He told Sheila that Abby was "history" because she refused to participate in the strongly recommended family therapy sessions. She figured that she wasn't real family so she wouldn't participate in the therapy. Because of this, Jake told her to get out.

This was the part of Jake that I had trouble trusting. It didn't go with his nature that he would send his girlfriend away because she wouldn't participate in therapy. After all, she wasn't real family and the State couldn't argue with that. Jake let her stay when she beat up and locked up his kids.

Jake had been involved with the system before. The system was a friend to him in some ways — it was familiar, fairly predictable, and sometimes there for him. Jake knew better than to talk the way he did to me, if he didn't want to get caught. His loneliness had caught up with him.

About a week after the contract had been in place, Candace's teacher told me this: "Candace was walking home from school and the crossing guard said, 'Candy, you look really sad?' and Candy said, 'That's because my daddy shot our dog.'"

I had to go check this out, so I went to Candy's classroom and all the kids were sitting in pods — little clusters of four desks pushed together. The children were spelling out b-l-a-c-k c-a-t. The teacher was demonstrating how to write the letter, "a." She said, "It's like a "c" with a zipper down its back."

It sounded like poetry, the way the teacher described making letters. "Black has two "ke" sounds," she said, "One with a c and one with a k. The k, boys and girls, is a straight back down with two branches — one reaching up to the sky and the other reaching down to the earth."

I sat next to Candace as she concentrated, gripping her fat pencil in her little hand, stopping every now and then to erase an errant line. When she was done, she beamed up at me, "Black cat," she said proudly.

The day before, I had visited a first grade room and had heard a primary teacher tell her class that, "Spiders can't be purple and the sun is not alive because it cannot reproduce and have babies." I saw the faces of the children, bewildered beyond questioning. I got up from my seat and left the room, closing the heavy door behind me.

I was more comfortable with the smell of spilled paste and letters with zippers down their backs. I enjoyed the pictures of children who colored out of the lines and drew purple spiders and blue pumpkins and green rain. I always liked visiting Candace's class.

Candace had remained in her seat when I had entered the

room during the writing lesson of "black cat." It was getting close to Halloween and the entire room was transformed with pumpkins and ghosts, spiders and black cats, made mostly out of different colors of construction paper. I was filled with joy to see that no two kids' pumpkins on the bulletin board looked alike.

Usually Candace bolted out of her seat or shot up from her carpet square on the floor when she saw me, no matter what the rest of the class was doing. Her eyes lit up in recognition when she saw me as if she knew instantly I was there to see her. I would come into the kindergarten room to see other kids too, but Candace knew that she had a premium on my attention.

I hadn't seen Candace since the interview with the case worker. I had seen more of her teacher in the faculty room or in the corridors. Her teacher had told me that Candy was "more aggressive lately."

"What is she doing?" I asked.

"Oh, taking things from kids. Well, actually, she is grabbing things out of the hands of other kids. She kicked another child for no reason. She ripped up another girl's paper for no reason."

One day, Candy's teacher caught me in the mail room and grabbed my arm. "I lied," she said. "I lied," she repeated. "Candace's dad came in this morning and surprised me. He asked me how she was doing. I said, 'Fine. She is doing just fine.' I didn't tell him about her behavior. The guy gave me the creeps. I was afraid that if I told him the truth, she would get punished."

❧ 📖 ❧

Candace shows me how she has written "black cat," on the rough paper with the wide-spaced lines. The paper is familiar to me. I remember the power surging through me when I wrote my own name for the first time kneeling on the living room floor, using the couch as a table, before anyone else in the house was awake. When my parents woke up, I showed them what I had done. That day, my mother took me to the library to get my own library card. I signed my name on the card. It was hard to squeeze all of the letters of my first and last name into such a small space. That card was my first known freedom.

Candace erases a bit of the "c" that is too closed, almost a complete circle. Satisfied with her work, she looks up at me and asks, "Can I come to your office now?"

I am surprised that she wants to come back. The last time we met in my office was when Child Protective Services came to do their investigation. I am relieved that Candace is not asking to come home with me as she has done in the past. I take this as a sign that she is feeling more secure in knowing that I am not going away, that I work at her school every week and on the weekend I go home just like she does. I say these things to comfort myself. Something is different. Something is wrong.

It is only Thursday. Maybe she reserves that overpowering need to go home with me for Friday. Fridays are not good days for Candace. It is on Fridays that she clings to the leg of her teacher's desk and refuses to let go.

Before we go to my office Candace tells me that she doesn't see her mother anymore, but drops things in her mailbox. I am aware of how strong the attachment can be for kids who have been mistreated and abused by their parents. They try even harder to please, hoping this time they will do it right and their parent will love them. These kids learn early on that love is conditional. It is something to be bargained for. There is no such thing as being valued just because they exist.

We bound off to my office, both dressed in purple and black, our ponytails bobbing behind us. We hold hands, delighted to be in each other's company.

Later, I will give Candace a heart cut out of construction paper. I will ask her for her favorite color and she will say, "You pick." Then she will say, "You write, 'I love you Candace,' on the heart that is your favorite color."

I choose purple. I add a sticker with a red apple on it and a rubber stamp pressed into a silver ink pad that makes a geometric design. I write the words, "I love you Candace," in black ink.

But before we end the session this way, with a keepsake, Candace directs the play and acts out themes of abandonment and fear and loneliness. Like so many, she has been misunderstood and hurt. I let her take charge. It is the only way that she knows how to get some semblance of control over the chaos that is her life.

Candace puts her hands on her hips and looks at the pictures of my own children on my desk. Her pupils seem to turn darker and cast accusation on me. "Are these your kids?"

Before I can answer, she orders me. "You are the mom and I am your girl and you love me." I wonder if I should take the pictures away from my desk; if they stir up too many feelings of loss for Candace. I let them stay.

"Mom, I need to go to the store to buy dog food," Candace announces. I am interested in her choice of dog food as the top item on her list considering what I have heard about her father shooting the dog.

"All right," I say, "but be back in one minute."

Candace skips around the office on her way to the store. She is like a toddler exploring a bigger world on her own and then returning to the safety of her "mother." We play this game for about ten minutes — she asks permission to go somewhere and I look at my watch and give her a precise time to return.

Next, Candace takes the dollhouse off of the shelf. "You got this for my birthday," she says.

"Yes." I say. "For you. Happy Birthday to my sweet daughter."

Candace opens the house and removes all of the small people.

"These are the neighbors. They are noisy and rude. They belong on the shelf." She places a handful of small people in a pile on the bookshelf. She leaves the large mother and father doll and the girl doll and the dog. She places the cat on top of the chimney, "This is the mom. She will sleep with me in the living room by the fireplace." Her features are composed as she concentrates. She is breathing audibly and steadily. "The dad goes on the roof," she announces.

"Oops," I say as the dad falls off of the roof and onto the far side of the table.

Candace leaves the dad alone. She is silent for a moment. She is still and I cannot hear her breath anymore.

"I wonder what happened to the dad?" I ask.

"He's dead," Candace says flatly. "A burglar came inside and killed him and threw him off of the roof and took the girl's allowance away."

Candace picks up the dead daddy doll and places him on the girl doll's lap. The daddy doll balances awkwardly in this position, his legs sticking out stiffly at right angles to the girl dolls outstretched legs.

"The daddy got killed," Candace reiterates. "He is a stuffed animal now. The girl plays with him."

Candace is now completely absorbed in her play. All the previous lightness has gone out of her from when we played "store," and she got permission to buy dog food.

Candace does not look at me when she makes these remarks about the dad and "the girl," talking about herself in the third person. I am careful to address her in character as "the girl" rather than Candace.

"The girl's father has been killed and now she has him to play with as a stuffed animal," I say.

Candace is staring. While she stares she manipulates the dolls. Because the daddy doll is now on "her" lap, the mother doll has been moved to the other side of the dollhouse living room where Candace has lined up three beds. The girl and the dad take up two beds and the little dog lies on the third bed. The mom has her back to this scene with her face pressed into the wall.

It is almost time for Candace to return to her classroom. I don't want to interrupt her play, but I need to know more about what happened to her real dog.

I address Candace by her real name and she startles out of her trance. I am sorry to steal her away from the delicious retreat her fantasy affords her.

"Candace, we have about five more minutes left. Candy?"

I have catapulted her back into the real world and she looks at me with her face screwed up. She is annoyed at me.

I sit across from Candace in a child's chair. Our knees are almost touching and she reaches out to lay her hands on top of mine. I turn my palms upward and we join hands.

"What happened to your dog?" I ask.

"My dad shot him in the backyard."

"Why?'

"Because Nick bit another dog and so my dad shot him. Nick was my favorite dog. He was our family dog. He didn't have to shoot him." Candy's voice is husky and tears come to her eyes. She is standing now, next to my chair, and I reach my arm around her waist. She falls easily into my lap.

"You must miss Nick terribly. You really loved Nick."

But Candace kicks my words aside, "My stupid mom gave away all the kittens, too. Now we have no one." She wipes at her eyes furiously with closed fists and will not cry. Then talks as if I am not in the room, "Do you think I really care? You're a nasty little brat. Go fuck yourself." Candace has left my lap and recites this litany of garbage language. Her teacher has told me that she has been doing this a lot lately in the home center of the classroom, too.

Abruptly, Candace turns to me. I notice that her hair has not been washed in awhile and her ponytail hangs limply to one side. Her face is chalk white and her eyes dark little stones. "Write," she commands me in a full voice. "Write. 'I love you Candace,' on a piece of paper."

While Candace cleans up the dollhouse, I pick out a heart and decorate it and write, "I love you Candace." She smiles when I hand her the heart and her two front teeth show black spots of decay. We clasp hands and I walk Candace back to her classroom.

She does not beg to come home with me today. There is a slowness in her walk that I have not seen before. She waves goodbye to me from her desk with her right hand and waves the paper heart, like a flag of surrender, in her left hand.

Tomorrow is Friday.

Therapy

A S A CHILD, I SAW A THERAPIST IN A MOVIE ONCE AND I WANTED to be her and I wanted her to heal me. The woman was large and expansive, draped in a loose fabric of South American design. Her face was tanned the color of warm sand and she had the most compassionate eyes set in this smooth unwrinkled face. I thought: this is god. This woman is god.

— 📖 —

When I go to my own therapist, it is because I have lost a child. I expect to stay for two sessions, max.

It has been nine months since I lost the child that was growing inside of me. My first therapy appointment is in the month when the child would have been born if it had not died inside my womb.

I worry about where my child is. What has happened to her since she left my body? I feel that this fragment of myself is out there floating around somewhere in the dark universe. I feel that this child was taken from me while I was sleeping. When I woke up, she wasn't there anymore and when I found out that she was gone, all I wanted to do was to sleep and sleep and never wake up again.

— 📖 —

My therapist is not a girl. I can see that right away. She is a woman. I feel safe with her right away. I cry most of the first session. In between my tears, I talk a little bit about my lost child. In the session, I am small and this missing girl is my little sister. I have left her somewhere.

I have dreams that I have left my child in a parking garage. I drive madly swerving up and down ramps, but I can never find her. I wake up sweating and afraid. I am not in my body. I hate my body. My body has betrayed me. My body has killed my child.

At the end of my first session, I fold myself into my therapist's arms. Her arms are strong and they can hold all my pain. I inhale her smell — a smell of simple things — cotton and soap. Her hair brushes my cheek.

I think that she is surprised when I hug her. I have talked mostly to the window during my first session.

Tucker

I SIT AT MY DESK STARING OUT THE WINDOW. I AM LOOKING FOR A focal point to steady myself. The ornamental maple with its rich burgundy leaves will satisfy. The tree is out of place among all the greenery. It cuts through the verdant jungle of summer's growth with passion. The tree is jarring. It is what I need to take me away from the persistent banging that occurs down the hall from my office. My door is shut, but the pounding persists on getting through.

I notice a rhythm to the boy's rage.

Tucker is in the in-school suspension room. The room is bare except for a metal garbage can which he heaves against the walls and ceiling until a staff person takes it away from him and holds the door shut from the outside with both of her hands. The pounding crescendos and then falls into a steady beat of fists against the door. I can hear his voice at times, "Bitch. Fuckin' bitch. Get off of me." They must be restraining him now.

The boy has "lost it" — as in lost control, lost his head, lost his marbles. He is pure emotion. Irrational. I'd like to trade places with him, but it is my job as a counselor not to lose it. I would like to yell and scream obscenities into that room until the walls could bear no more.

Today, Tucker does not give up. He butts the door with his shoulder. The door opens for an instant and I can hear his breath heavy with words that infiltrate the school's corridors like a poisonous gas.

The door is quickly slammed shut by the two staff standing guard. The staff laugh and joke about being prison guards. They laugh because they are afraid, afraid of this undistilled emotion.

I am doing battle inside my body. I stare at the ornamental maple. It is a cloudy day and the tree looks garish against the backdrop of gray sky. I admire Tucker for his fight. I feel like a coward.

The banging and pounding persists, cascading with the force of a million waterfalls that churn and foam out of that little room, tearing down the walls of this well-ordered school.

Alex

I SAW ALEX TODAY. SHE WAS SITTING IN THE NURSE'S OFFICE, HER back very straight, her hands folded in her lap. But the first thing I noticed about Alex was that her hair was gone. The golden curls that used to bounce all over her head and sneak out from under her cap in a riot of corkscrew madness, were gone. Her hair had been clearcutted and in its place, a brown stubble was growing in.

Alex looked years older with her curls gone, though she was only six and starting kindergarten a year late. She still wore the same round, wire-rim glasses that gave her a studious look. Alex looked like she was meditating when I peeked into the door of the nurse's office.

We had known each other two years earlier, when she had come to the therapeutic center I was working in then. She was four. She was bright. Her parents were disabled: tested out with low I.Q.'s, had trouble picking up cues, like when to feed or change the diaper of the younger baby when he cried.

Alex's mom was functionally illiterate. She signed her name with an "X" and a little squiggle. One day Alex's mom told me that she wanted to learn to read and write so she could keep up with Jimmy. Jimmy was her husband.

I didn't think she was serious about the reading and writing thing, but she kept asking me until I took her to the library and helped her to enroll in a literacy class.

We all thought that there would come a time when Alex would become cognizant of the fact that she was brighter, way brighter, than both of her parents. That imminent transition worried the staff but, at age four, never entered Alex's mind.

As I looked again at Alex in the nurse's office, I thought maybe her demeanor wasn't one of meditation, but rather depression. She was six now, almost seven, the age of reason when a child can begin to see themselves as individual, seperate from, and in relation to, others. I wondered if she knew.

When I approached Alex, who was perched on the edge of the nurse's cot, she flinched a little and continued to look straight ahead when I talked to her. She flashed a smile when I said I had known her as a much younger girl. She allowed me to sit beside her, and I was careful not to touch her. Then I noticed the smell — the rank and sour odor of fecal material that has been there for a while.

Alex had been encopretic (making bowel movements in places other than the toilet) for many days: 9/4, 9/7, 9/12… the dates continued, listed in Alex's school medical chart with a brief, written description next to them. "Child came to school already smelling." "Child must have soiled herself during circle time — sent to nurse to get cleaned up." There were twelve incidences in all.

The odor emanating from Alex was overpowering. I didn't want to get up abruptly or say anything to embarrass her. The nurse told me that she was getting teased by the rest of the class, and that no one would play with Alex because of her smell. The nurse also said that Alex came to school hungry and had lost weight.

I got on the phone and called Alex's teacher from last year. She had gone to a special pre-K class to ready her for regular kindergarten. It had been a hard decision to retain her. She knew her shapes and colors. She was articulate and loved to learn.

The problem was her behavior. Alex would throw tantrums if she didn't get to play with what she wanted. At times, she would laugh at what the teacher thought were "inappropriate times."

When the school bus arrived to take Alex home, she would go limp and refuse to ride. The bus driver and the teacher's aide had to carry her on to the bus and strap a seatbelt around her in the seat right behind the driver.

The nurse put Alex's dirty clothes in a plastic bag. I thought of the little girl carrying her bag home like a sack of dead meat.

The next day, Alex was referred to my office for counseling. I went to get her in her classroom, and she came readily, skipping down the corridor, holding onto my hand. Her jawbone was well defined without the sprigs of curls around it and she had the face of an owl; a sharp little nose and crystalline blue eyes that focused from behind her glasses.

We sat and looked at each other for a few minutes. Then Alex said, "I'm hungry." I foraged around my desk to give her something to eat and came up with an apple, which she accepted. Alex chewed on the apple and I tried to reestablish a relationship with her.

I knew she loved dolls, so I pulled out the family of small dolls I had and she immediately asked me to get down the dollhouse, too. Alex played with the dolls and put the father doll on the bookshelf.

"He doesn't belong in the family," she announced.

"Why is that," I asked?

"He's a bad boy."

Alex continued to play with the dolls and the house, rearranging furniture, and making up a swimming pool with a piece of blue construction paper for the mother and the children to splash around in. Her play was controlled, but imaginative. I watched. We didn't talk much.

About halfway through the session I noticed the smell of feces again. I asked Alex if she needed to use the bathroom. She shook her head no. The smell was so obvious I thought to avoid discussion on this topic would be to cover up, act like nothing was going on, which happened so much for her in her family and with other adults. I asked her directly, "Did you poop your pants? It's okay. Everyone has accidents now and then."

Alex avoided my question. She looked away from me and eventually turned all the way around in her chair.

I asked Alex how things were going at home.

She said, "Fine."

I reminded her that it was okay to say anything in my room.

That I was the only one here listening. Her parents were not in this room. Her teacher was not in this room. Just me and my toys.

Alex would not budge. I told her that we needed to walk down the hall to the nurse's office so she could get cleaned up before going back to class. She got up from her chair, still not looking at me. I put my hand on her shoulder and she let me. She said, "I'm stinky. I'm stinky."

I said, "Poop is stinky, but *you* are not stinky. You are Alex and I like you a lot."

I dropped Alex off at the nurse's office and returned to my office to call her teacher from last year.

Her former teacher told me this: Last year Alex had soiled a few times a week. There had been a report to Child Protective Services around a disclosure Alex had made while in the bathroom. She had said, "It burns." She had gone on to describe her father washing her "inside there with his fingers." The case had been investigated and closed. The caseworker must have ignored the words of the five year old. The caseworker must have forgotten that encopresis is often associated with severe trauma such as sexual abuse. Alex's father promised not to take showers with her anymore and that was the end of it.

I hung up the phone and thought about Alex.

Her short history of six years was certainly on a linear course. At four, she was bouncy and bright and always used the toilet. At five she had bright days and dark days, about half and half, her former teacher had said. At five and a half, Alex had "an accident" in her pants about four or five times a month.

At six, it was all dark days and a lot of "accidents."

The school principal told me to report this information about Alex to Child Protective Services. I felt the weight of my responsibility and the plunge into hopelessness as I knew the system was not set up to truly help families. Parents almost always viewed the system as punitive. Even if they were given free services, negotiating the maze of paperwork and appointments could be overwhelming. Transportation was often an issue. Bus fare could mean going without milk for a few days.

I called and was put on hold. I waited and was told they were too busy to take my call right now. I said, "I have to leave here in fifteen minutes to pick up my own children," and they said, "Okay. Hold on." In a few seconds a woman picked up the line and took down the information about Alex. I waited until the end of the call for her to say, "Well, this is not really enough to investigate."

I pressed on with the history. The family lived in a crowded one room apartment. They rarely went out. The kids got to see the parks and the zoo only on school field trips. I mentioned again about the lack of food and the parent's disabilities that prevented them from accessing services. The worker paused for a moment and then said, "All right, I'll send a public health nurse over there." I breathed out in relief. These small victories could make or break my day.

A couple of weeks later I saw Alex in the hall on her way to gym. She did not bounce or smile, but she did not look unhappy either. It looked like Alex was saving up all of her energy for something big that might happen later. She observed everything without comment. She nodded when she saw me and gave me a little smile.

I thought I saw a protective cloud around Alex, preserving her. Her teacher pulled me aside and said, "Alex has been clean a week and a half now."

Summer School

ALEX IS WAITING OUTSIDE OF THE MAILROOM DOOR WITH EVE (the teaching assistant assigned to Alex by the school). When Alex sees me come through the door, she lets out a big, "ahhhh," and I crouch down to hug her. Alex wraps her arms around me and says, "When do I get to go with you?" She has gotten thinner and the stained wrap-around skirt she is wearing falls well below her knees and looks like it has been wrapped twice around her waist and is still too big. Ever since the lice infestation, Alex's parents have kept her hair closely cropped delineating the contours of her skull.

I am worried about Alex. Summer is coming and it will be like a life sentence to this child. Eve and I decided to visit the family's one bedroom apartment during the last week of school.

Jeanette, Alex's mom, said, "Just park in back behind the adult game and video shop and then walk around to the back. We're in B101." I knew where the place was. I had driven by the apartments often. A year ago there had been a fire and I was surprised to see the building nearly destroyed and within days built up again to city safety codes.

Eve and I met at the Kendall's residence. I was glad I had parked behind the porno shop because the driveway to the back door (the only door) to the apartment was littered with shards of broken beer bottles, cigarette butts, and fast food wrappers. The dumpster was overflowing and, because the day was sultry, the smell of rotten decay was overpowering.

Alex was out the door in shorts and no shirt before we could knock.

She jumped into Eve's arms and then asked me, "What did you bring for me?" Alex was used to social workers coming to the house bringing various toys and games for educational purposes. I had a bunch of colored markers and handed those over to Alex who reminded me it was her birthday in a few weeks and would I come to her party.

Jeanette hung in the background absentmindedly dragging a brush through her hair. Her stomach protruded over black stretch pants and out from under the cropped top she was wearing.

"Alex. You're spoiled. Spoiled rotten," she said, when I gave the child the markers and a pad of paper to draw on. By the end of the visit, Alex had written her ABC's for Eve and had made me a colorful picture. "This is me, typing inside a butterfly," she said.

Jeanette continued to stroke her hair with the brush. In between strokes she would stare at the big screen T.V. and exclaim with delight when she recognized a band member on MTV. The rhythm to her hair brushing was peculiar, almost unconscious. She must have brushed for a half an hour and when she was done there were still large masses of tangles in the back. Unlike her daughter, Jeanette wore her hair long and frizzy. Where it grew out at the roots, I noticed some streaks of gray.

I looked around for a place to sit and uncovered a small square on the end of the sofa. I sat next to a blue lace bra, several T-shirts in need of washing and an unemptied cat box that had spilled some of its contents onto the heaps of stuff on the sofa. I was assaulted with the chaos that basic survival can generate. Although the one-room place, with a small sleeping alcove for Alex and her baby brother, was as large as a medium sized dining room, the place was covered with mounds of clothing for all seasons, broken bicycles, umbrellas, disposable diapers, dirty dishes, crucifixes, and small parcels of garbage stashed into plastic grocery bags.

Eve decided to stand as did Jeanette. Alex sat on the floor using up the entire pad of paper I had given her. She asked if she could keep the markers and I said, "They're yours."

It was wonderful to watch Alex delight in simple pleasures. I had seen her so desolate for so long. Opening the door to company was a big deal for her and she glowed with a peaceful happiness I had not seen in a long time.

Eve asked to see where Alex slept. Alex led Eve to her "room," the space she shared with her younger brother. Two twin beds were jammed together and the sheets were stained with brown spots and badly needed washing. The floor was covered with clothing and a few broken plastic toys.

While Alex and Eve were in the back bedroom, Jeanette and I hammered out what would be a workable summer school schedule for Alex. Since the family didn't have a car, getting Alex to school entailed walking her to a bus stop about a half mile away — a fair challenge for her parents who were both disabled with vision problems and cognitive delays. It was difficult for them to read a bus schedule, and I spent fifteen minutes going over what time to set the alarm and what time to leave the house to get Alex to the bus stop on time.

Jeanette got quite flustered with the details of scheduling and we had to stop for awhile and watch MTV while she let her mind absorb the information most of us are all too adept at handling — scheduling everything to the last minute. For a moment I admired the simplicity and complexity of this family structure. They were making it work. Whatever they were doing, the kids were getting fed and clothed and had better shelter than many places I had been. When I told Jeanette what a good job she was doing she deferred to her husband, "He's the one with the brains. I told you. He's the one who takes care of all this," and she gestured toward yet more paperwork that needed to be filled out in order for Alex to be considered for a summer school scholarship.

Eve and I left after about an hour and Alex made us promise that we would come to her birthday party. She would be turning seven in August.

Out in the parking area, that was really an extension of the dumpster, I breathed in deeply despite the stench that wafted through the air. The apartment had felt claustrophobic, and I couldn't imagine living in the chaos that the Kendall family lived in.

I felt that Alex would survive. She was smarter than her parents and helped read forms for her mother. Alex's older sister had been placed in guardianship by the state and then adopted by a friend of the family. I had never met Jennifer, but I knew it was an open adoption and Alex saw her sister often.

The state had been involved with the Kendall family on and off for years and it was only a few months ago that another report had been filed by a neighbor on alleged neglect of Alex and her baby brother, Joseph, who played out back among the litter, unsupervised and would show up at the doors of neighbors asking for food.

Alex was smart and she was spirited. Although she could fall to the depths of desolation, she could also come bouncing out with an electric energy that was contagious. I hoped to see Alex grow up and grow strong.

The Kids Today

I SEE ALEX AT SCHOOL. SHE RARELY MISSES A DAY. SHE GREETS ME with the same smile that spreads slowly like warm molasses. She has become a friend of Candace. They are both in first grade now. Their favorite game is playing house. They sit at their desks working and spring up when the recess bell rings so that they can continue their elaborate game of house. Sometimes Candace is the dad, and sometimes Alex is the dad, or one or the other of them is the baby. They trade roles around and their play evokes either happy fantasies or real life scenarios that happened yesterday, a month ago, a year ago.

Candace still buys dog food for her imaginary dog. Alex is almost seven. She corrects her mother's homework papers from the literacy class she is taking. Alex has grown tall and strong. She is a good friend for Candace.

I keep expecting to see Sally at the grocery store or riding her bike in the street. Her family moved again after the trailer they were living in was condemned. I don't know where she is, but I know I will see her some day.

My brother is heavily medicated. He was recently released from a psychiatric hospital. I speak to him once in awhile on the phone, but he is inaccessible. His words come strung together, and I cannot delineate where he begins and where his illness ends.

The State funding for another child I've been working with has run out. He will transfer to a new therapist. It is yet another separation for him, however, this time it will be done gently and the trust he has learned in his therapy thus far will transfer over to the new therapist. That is the hope.

PART V

FIERCE WITH REALITY

"You need to claim the events of your life to make yourself yours.
When you truly possess all you have been and done
which may take some time, you are fierce with reality."
—Florida Scott Maxwell

Julian

THEY COME TO ME WITH THEIR MILK TEETH STILL INTACT. THE ones who have started healing bring me things: a dime and a penny; a crumpled, crayoned picture; a pebble from the road. The ones who aren't healing want to take things from my office and, if I won't let them, they ball up in a corner on the floor and cry or refuse to look at me for the rest of the session.

It is always their smells that get to me: little ones with musty powdery smells hanging around them like some kind of angel aura. Even the children with urine-soaked pants and smudged faces smell good. The crowns of their heads still unformed in my mind like those of tiny babies. My hand gravitates to that spot.

Their diagnosis doesn't matter so much. To me, they come for comfort and love — what any child comes to an adult for. That's all I have to give them anyway. That I am a child therapist doesn't make a bit of difference to a four year old. They address me as "Martha" or "Mom" or "flower" or "friend." I am a doe or a dragon, a demon or a murderer depending on what they are playing out at the time. I am kissed, kicked, spit on and hugged till I almost choke. Always, the kids get to me in the same way. They break my heart.

Our country gives out Ritalin to children and manufactures peppermint-flavored Prozac for them. Childhood has become a disorder. In a world where so many children are shuttled off to poor quality daycare and other programs, perhaps we need to look at a disorder called "Parental Attention Deficit."

The insurance companies authorize "brief, solution-oriented treatment" across the board. That is not treatment. A traumatized child cannot be expected to heal in ten sessions, the average amount of sessions allowed under most insurance plans. Crime Victims wants a mountain of paperwork if the child does not respond in three sessions. Then you might get six more and a few more after that, but it is always a battle fighting for your client's right and need for treatment.

As my frustration with the system grows, I find I can no longer function within it and feel that I am providing sound and ethical treatment. I decide to set up a private practice in north Seattle so that I can stay with my clients until they are ready to move on — even if it means using a sliding fee scale.

We're coming to the end of our sessions and, still, he draws himself and a salmon, and they look the same. Julian pinches his thumb and index finger around an orange marker and applies the point to the newsprint pad with the precision of a graphic artist. The lines coalesce on the page and look nothing like a boy or a salmon. Each week we meet, Julian repeats this pattern as if for the first time. The shapes are eerie and remind me of amoebas.

When I look at Julian's work, a dullness settles through me. Usually I feel a rush when I observe a child's primary process: their raw, uncensored work that comes from a place that can be felt and not explained. With Julian, it's only dust.

Julian divides each figure asymmetrically with a horizontal slash that could be the mouth or the waist or a belt. I don't ask. I say, "Tell me about your drawings," and sometimes he does and most times he doesn't and I don't know what the horizontal slash is all about.

The shapes are bottom heavy with a little point at the top, resembling a raindrop with eyes and a certain fashion of arms that look more like spikes. I look hard, but can see no evidence of legs. I take in the boy. He appears calm and focused, almost feminine in his receptivity.

The drawings leave me cold, but the boy encourages me by the way he bends into his work with such certainty. The way he says with conviction, "I draw me. Now I draw a salmon," and grazes me with the flash of a smile that lingers on his full red lips.

— 📖 —

There is nothing single-minded about my job as a therapist. It's about left brain and right brain, intuition, and textbook theory, and rational and irrational thoughts that take me down untraveled paths.

What's left of the afternoon is becoming early winter night. I see myself reflected in my double-pane windows with yellowed paint peeling around the frames. I look rather plain in a navy blue turtleneck sweater and corduroy skirt. I am a construction worker. I tear people down and build them up again.

I sip lukewarm coffee, watch the night sky swallow the last slice of silver light and study the drawings of a child not quite six, dubbed "disturbed" by all accounts professional and otherwise. I peruse the drawings straight on as I have for eight weeks and then turn them upside down and sideways and no matter which way I turn the boy/salmon the dullness remains, weighing me down. I wish for the crispness of an acute emotion like sadness or anger or joy, feelings that come alive and grow and eventually die. Feelings that have a natural life cycle, but when I look at these pictures, I'm stuck in limbo.

I keep thinking that the boy and the salmon belong in the same body and one day they will come together to form a healthy, human-looking picture. The picture of the boy has fists, which indicate a power fueled by anger.

Julian is small for his six years and the perishable quality that surrounds many children like an aura is exaggerated on him because of his size and delicate bone structure. At times Julian is so lucid I can see into him for miles. At other times he fades until he disappears and cannot be pulled out of the hat.

On the inside, Julian seems to be experiencing a meltdown of sorts. His "passivity," his lack of interest in "normal boy things," his insistence on doing things "in his own way on his own time," are simply "little problems of growing up," that I have been hired to fix. Julian shows little spontaneity. In eight weeks I have not heard his laugh. He no longer plays so hard that he forgets my prescence.

In our third session, Julian surprises me by assigning me the role of his dad and gives me the script to go along with my character. "Say, 'Where'd you get those?'" he directs me.

So I say, "Julian, where'd you get those markers?"

And he answers, "At the store."

Then Julian cues me for my next line, "You stole them! Here's a surprise for you!" And takes out the toy gun, hands it to me, and tells me to shoot him. Then he takes the gun and shoots himself. I don't want to end the session that way so I play "rescue" and try to fix Julian up with the doctor's kit, but he won't let me touch him or put a Band-Aid on. He wants to do all the fixing up himself.

I show him some cards with stick figures in different feeling states. He picks the "love" card and tells me this story: "He was laughing and he feeled his heart and he was walking and he was happy about something. He was about to go to the park." Julian picks out one more card before leaving, the one that is labeled "hurt," and tells me this story: "He was trying to go somewhere and he was mad because his mom told him that he wasn't supposed to go to the park."

In our fourth session, Julian came into the play area and got the white adhesive tape out of the toy medical kit. He used up most of the roll of tape. He taped over the eyes and the ears and the mouth of the teddy bear and left it to sit in a little chair alone for the remainder of the session. As the bear sat deaf, mute, and blind, Julian talked. He told me how he loved strawberry ice cream and playing his Nintendo. He wished for a baby brother and thought he might still get one even though his parents were splitting up. He told me something about a trip to the locks back then, but it hadn't seemed significant at the time. He finished his monologue with: "When it is too hot, the ice cream melts and then I can't have it because it could ruin my clothes. We can't have a puppy because he could chew my mom's shoes and pee the floor. What kind of ice cream do you like?"

I had felt so much wild frenetic energy in that one exchange and I wanted to run with Julian on that electricity forever, but it was over as soon as it began. He had said, "We saw the fish, the big fish. We saw them. The big ones." I had said, "Tell me more, Julian. Tell me more about the fish, the salmon fish," but he had turned from me then. He had gone to the blocks and built a tower and then knocked it down.

I try to imagine what it must be like living inside Julian's mind and I can't. I put my coat on and turn out the lights before stepping into the coolness of night and breathe in drafts of damp snowy air that reminds me of how numb my hands could get as a child in wet woolen mittens, and how the wool smelled like hay when the mittens were hung out to dry in front of the fire.

It had been snowing a wet Northwestern snow off and on, the first time I met Julian and his mother. The presence of the thin white blanket with blades of brown and green grass piercing through, quieted the outer world.

I am sifting through my reasons and motives for becoming a therapist and coming up blank. The intrigue of hooking clues together that often ended in an unsolved or partially solved mystery? The power of reconstructing the human heart without the precision of an exact science to guide me? I did the work because the children talked to me and that was worth a lot.

For the next five weeks, Julian replicated the salmon/boy picture like a recurring dream. "I draw a salmon. Now I draw me. The salmon cannot swim."

When Julian worked on his drawings, the skin over his forehead and cheekbones turned pale and tight and drawn. His breath came slow and heavy: in through his nose and out through his parted lips with a long whoosh of resignation. At times he inhaled so deeply that the force of the air shook his slight frame, and he shuddered like a fragile vessel that could easily fracture. As Julian drew, the outer world fell away, and if I called out his name he did not acknowledge that he had heard me.

When he was done, Julian capped the orange marker and

held it between his thumb and two middle fingers rolling it back and forth. Eventually, his breath came in gentle waves in and out of his nose and he would often fall asleep with his soft curls resting against the hardwood of the table.

As he slept, I studied the shapes. Primitive. Crude. Unsettling. The orange color was reminiscent of napalm, insect repellent lights screwed into rotting porch ceilings, antiseptic solution, not a primary color.

For six weeks of therapy, it was orange marker, newsprint pad and two nearly identical shapes. I tried to engage Julian with puppets and the sand tray, but mostly it was just the drawing and not much conversation.

At our seventh meeting, Julian curled his fingers around the loose fabric of my corduroy skirt and pressed his cheek into my leg hard enough to leave imprints from the corduroy on his face. I stroked his hair and reached down to feel his soft curls. The steady pressure of his silence was palpable like a physical pain. I was afraid that if I held him, he could not tolerate the closeness and would squirm away.

I wanted only to uncover his truth and free him from an unreasonable exile, but I knew how high the stakes ran. A child so sensitive could die on the outside, like a domesticated animal set loose, all at once, in the wild.

— 📖 —

It's our second-to-last session and I ask Julian to tell me about his drawings again. His skin has become dull with dryness over the last few months and he has lost weight, but his voice is strong and melodic. "This is me. I'm sad. Now I draw a salmon."

I'm not getting the connection between the boy and the salmon. I take another swallow of cold coffee and don't realize I have done so until I taste its bitterness. I think of breaking through the boy's silence in the way a ship plows its hull indiscriminately through smooth and icy waters or a surgeon cracks through breastbone to reach the heart.

After today, we have only one session left. Ten therapy sessions. That is the amount of time I have to fix a child. "Fix," as in repair. "Fix," as in freeze in time. Arrest the emotional damage that grows unchecked like the ugliest of cancers. I hold the image of the child in my mind as a photograph steeped in a chemical bath, but the solution is not right. He is not developing in the correct amount of time.

Perhaps I have been too gentle in my approach. I push my coffee cup away annoyed at myself for lack of progress. I lean forward on my elbows, and rest my chin on my hands until my face is even with Julian's face, a face small and shrunken like an old man's. His nose and mouth are finely sculpted under a broad forehead. His skin flakes in places, and I want to rub cream into his cheeks to bring out a lovely, warm luster.

I am so near to Julian that I can smell the sweetness of childhood like heat and summer and earth coming from the boy's skin, his hair, his clothing. Julian is turned slightly away from me, poised with a primal grace. He shows little reaction to my physical closeness, a slight pinch of muscle between his dark eyebrows and a folding in of his shoulders like protective angel's wings. His eyes are lucid with a greenish tint to the irises.

I sit in despair before this small person, the one whose mother calls him "baby" and repeats the mantra, "I know you can do better than that, honey," a thousand times a day. I warm my coffee mug between my own strong hands and close my eyes imagining it is Julian that I am cradling between my palms like a baby sparrow.

While I am thinking, Julian gets up and takes the tablecloth off of the child's picnic table and encases himself in a plastic cocoon. He returns to the table and rests his head in the crook of his elbow. He allows me to rub his back. I can hear the wall clock's steady buzz and the rasp of my shirt cuff against the plastic covering as I move my hand up and down the arc of Julian's back.

Our heads are touching across the table as I continue to rub Julian's back. Somehow I am hoping that he will read my intention by osmosis. "I thought you would have been healed more by now. I thought I could have uncovered your essence and found it to be smooth and still like water. I hoped you would have shot forth brightly colored blossoms and filled out in the hollow places, your cheeks, your belly, your soul. I thought I would have touched you more by now."

When I open my eyes, they are wet. If Julian notices, I can't tell.

"Julian, we have five more minutes. Is there anything more you want to say today before you leave?" I am damming back a wall of tears.

Julian balls his fists into his eyes in answer to my question or in recognition of my tears. Sunlight patterns the floor through the slats of the Venetian blinds, but I feel like it is evening. I have the sensation of having swum under water for a very long time. I am exhausted. I want to title my final report, "The Splitting of a Child: A Mutated Result of Misguided Parental 'Love.'"

"Julian," I plead, "talk to me. Tell me more about the salmon, about your sadness." My voice splinters into shavings of frustration, anger, sorrow.

Julian presses his spine into the back of his chair and folds his hands into his lap. He whispers, "Fish don't have hands. Can't swim." He annunciates the words precisely and delicately as if they might break. I am afraid to push too hard. I sit back and wait.

The stifling of a child's soul is the most painful experience to witness and I see that going on with Julian. He is suffocating and I am trying to dig him out, but I am afraid to really pull him out because he might unravel in my arms like a mummy. I think that maybe I should be digging harder, but I'm not sure.

Julian is talking. We have one session left after this and he is talking. "The big fish. The salmon fish, I saw them. Their eyes were like this," and Julian makes his own eyes wide and bulging.

"Tell me more about what you saw."

"They didn't swim. They were stuck there. I put my hands on the glass. Go fish! But they stayed there."

"What happened next?" Julian is staring, remembering. "Julian. What happened next with the fish?"

Julian's voice becomes soft, but tense with anger, "What's the matter with you … what's the matter with you?" He is shaking now. His eyes are rimmed with tears that don't spill.

"Who is talking?" I ask. "Who is saying these things?"

Julian is gesturing with his fists, pounding the air. His pupils are dilated. His voice cracks with emotion. His words pulse fast and then slow. "Daddy," he sobs. "Daddy, please, help the fish. Help them get out. Their eyes…"

"What about their eyes?" I ask.

"Eyes open. Don't shut," Julian replies. "They can't sleep in the trap."

"What happened at the locks, Julian?"

The child is crying openly now. "My daddy, he pulled me like this." Julian grabs himself by the shoulders. "He said, 'Get a hold of yourself.' He slapped me on the mouth."

I can see the fish, their eyes bulging caught in the fish ladders, too tired to make it upstream. The child trying to save the fish. The father disturbed by his son's sensitivity. The image of the salmon, exhausted and vigilant looks a lot like Julian to me. This boy with the pounding fists aborted in his mission to free what he saw as something entrapped.

I go home, heat a frozen chicken pie and, after eating it, decide to go for a swim. The public pool turns off its overhead lights for the eight to nine p.m. adult "stress-buster" swim. Under the water I open my eyes and the color is an intense aquamarine like you see in cartoons. I swim one length kicking my legs as hard as I can and swim back in a smooth breaststroke taking even breaths of air each time my arms sweep open the water and allow my head to surface. My muscles relax in the cool water. My breathing becomes deep and rhythmic and I finish with a long, easy, back float. I float with my eyes closed until I lose all track of time and space. My body meshes with the water until there is no boundary. I want to stay this way forever.

When the guards flick on the lights a jet of adrenalin shoots through my heart, down through my belly, and turns my legs to jelly. I climb out of the pool. As I dress, I think of Julian and how the water would envelop and hold him and he would swim underwater, his hair streaming back, with a thousand strong salmon.

—　📖　—

It is our last session. I have told Julian that our time will be ending. I hate the pain of separating from Julian.

Julian chooses a fat black crayon. I expect something big to happen. He is going to describe for me the texture and temperature of his interior world. He will draw out his pain like a poison and be healed.

Julian draws a stick figure that looks female. There is a triangle for a skirt and two spindly legs. He traces over the figure, glances up at me and returns to focus on the head of the girl or the woman he is drawing. I recognize my own dangly earrings.

Next, Julian draws a heart. This black, misshapen heart is placed outside of the woman's body in the upper left corner of the page like a return address. Julian concentrates hard on the heart, grinding the crayon down to a nub, going over and over the outline, surrounding the heart with a thick rind. I smell the heavy scent of wax and paper, crayon shavings that lie in small curls around the edge of the paper.

Watching Julian work this way scares me. I am lost in a blinding wall of panic that hits me broadside. My thoughts tangle and I feel dizzy. The picture is of me. I cannot reconcile this rendition of myself.

"Heartless," I say to myself.

Julian must think that I've given up on him. How else would he interpret "termination," the clinical term for concluding therapy? I want to tell him to put my heart back inside my body with a jagged line through it because right now it is breaking.

Julian finishes the picture of me and puts his initials, "J.H.," in the lower right corner of the paper. He puts the drawing of me into my outstretched hand, and I begin to cry with a fullness that I have not felt before. A fullness that cannot be emptied. I feel his breath, clean and odorless and cool against my cheek.

"How I see you, Julian, is as a spirit inside a heart inside a body. I love you. I will hold you here," I say motioning to my heart. I take up a pencil and draw an outline. It is a simple line drawing of myself as a child. Julian says, "You look like an angel."

I add waves of dark hair, strong hands, long legs and feet that reached to the middle of the page and give me the appearance of floating in space. I draw a heart with the initials, "J.H.," inscribed inside the heart inside my body. I don't know if he understands my words that are erupting from some primitive place inside of me. I am talking through my tears. Julian is listening. His eyes are ignited with brightness.

Julian takes the picture and folds the paper until it is small enough to fit into his pants pocket. I don't know if Julian understands my words, but I know that against his pain, he is pushing up like a strong green shoot through the cracked earth and I do not want to stop him.

A Baker

BEFORE I BECAME A CHILD THERAPIST, I WORKED DOWNTOWN AS A baker. I was in charge of making all the breads for the sandwiches. When I got to work at five in the morning, the man who baked cinnamon rolls was just finishing up his shift, removing large trays of gooey rolls from the oven and setting out the plastic tables and chairs in the courtyard for the customers that would fill the bakery by seven.

I lived simply then. I rode my rusty, brown Atalia up and down the hilly city streets with a pack on my back, one pant leg held tight by a rubber band so it wouldn't get stuck in my bicycle chain. The kitchen of the bakery I worked in was downstairs in this historic building made of red brick and covered with ivy in the old part of town. It appealed to my romantic sensibilities.

Looking back now, I think my job as a baker prepared me more than anything else to become a therapist. To bake, you have to be fully present. You have to put love into your work or it doesn't come out right. You have to learn patience and precision. You have to listen and feel and respond. You have to have a heart.

I developed this kind of relationship with the bread I baked and it was the best in the city: crusty loaves of black rye and wheat and sourdough. I could make anything the customer wanted: French baguettes, croissants, or twelve-grain dinner rolls.

The mixer was huge, big enough for a small child to hide in. I poured tens of cups of flour at a time into this vat, cubes of fresh yeast that had warmed and bubbled in baths of tepid water, and honey or oats or fresh rosemary and thyme for herb breads. The giant hook on the mixer did the hard work of blending twenty pounds of dough and, when it was done, I dug my hands into the bowl and thunked five pounds of dough at a time onto the smooth wooden table. Usually the radio was playing and my hands worked in rhythm to its beat, kneading with my palms, turning the dough a quarter turn and kneading again until the dough was smooth and elastic and its warm brown surface let me know it was ready to rest.

I lay out ten, two-pound balls of dough at a time on the table and, covering them with a cotton cloth, allowed them to rise in the heat of the kitchen. While they were rising I took a coffee break and watched the cook build his salads with the meticulous care of a Zen gardener. In fact, the cook was Zen and was often in trouble for getting the food up to the café late, he took so much care and attention to his work.

In this kitchen, everything was simple. The bread never gave me any trouble. It always turned out right.

Treatment

I HAVE BEEN COMING TO SEE JAN FOR ALMOST A YEAR NOW AND I still disappear sometimes. Jan leans forward in her chair trying to make contact with me. "So let me ask you this? How much are you in your body right now?"

She has noticed. Someone has found me out. I look for places in my therapist's office to hide. Finding none, I cry. Big, slow tears heavy with my entrapment.

I've been caught. I have nowhere to go, but deeper inside as the tears sting my eyes and humiliate me.

My whole body is numb. I can't look up to get a Kleenex because she might see me. The grief of a hundred years builds up in me. I start to feel something; a red hot poker in my solar plexus. I mark my discomfort by passing my palm over the area just below my rib cage.

I can feel Jan's presence steady and aware. I want to cross over to her side, but I feel too weak. All of my energy is collapsing inward.

I still haven't answered her question — "How much are you in your body now?"

We were talking about sex. At least that's the last thing I remember talking about until Jan's voice began to fade from my range of hearing, and I began to cover myself and hide myself within myself. I answer, "I don't know." I speculate to myself — maybe thirty-three percent ... twenty-two percent ... present?"

I can hide so fast you wouldn't even know that I had left. I can change quicker than a chameleon. You will never find me if I turn myself as

white as the sheets. You will not know that I am gone. At ten years old,
I won't know that either. It will take me years of therapy to find out
where I have gone.

I've kept my hair the same since I was a teenager. It's thinner now and specked with gray. The systems in my body are amazingly strong to withstand the constant assault of adrenalin that moves through me with the force of pistons pumping and pumping. When I run hard or swim fast, a valve opens and adrenalin flows out in a sticky, yellow river. On the inside, a lock down can occur at any time with or without warning — it's automatic. Things that trigger traumatic memories trip the system and cause an all-body lock down.

The brain gets the same treatment. Thinking, concentrating, and focusing become dull, the brain a useless instrument.

The surges of the catecholmines — the body's stress chemicals, become stronger and poke my muscles like a trillion needles. I can't feel anything except nausea. I can't focus my eyes. It's like everyone can see you, but you can't see them. An acute state of self-consciousness occurs — a feeling like your body is wrapped in green wool and your mouth is filled with sand.

Panic. Try to find the door. Enter a room and look for all possible
escape routes. Avoid elevators and small, windowless rooms — they
intensify the effect of claustrophobia. There's no way out. Someone could
be coming up behind you.

My brother has become a stranger. He stands naked at my door
exposing himself to me. I am ten. For six years, I lock down so that I am
blind to his erection, his wild black hair, and his black eyes — his
stalking. I am blind.

After my brother leaves my room, I struggle to find myself. I am lost.
I can't get back.

Every time I am with a man, I feel this same way.

The clinical name for what I am experiencing is called Post Traumatic Stress Disorder. When I first find out that I have this disorder, I am relieved because now it has a name.

Bed

I TRY TO SLEEP. THE WIND REMINDS ME OF TURMOIL. THE STICKS AND leaves and dirt on the ground get all mixed up with the swirling air. Nothing is where it belongs. Everything is out of place. The wind unsettles me. It has been blowing around inside of me all of my life.

The ocean breathes. The waves come tumbling onto shore in a giant exhale. The receding waves rumble in a soft inhale. The ocean's breath is comforting. I like the rhythm.

I go to sleep now with the music of the ocean playing through headphones and a hot water bottle wrapped inside a flannel pillowcase pressed to my solar plexus.

The music and the warm flannel lull me to sleep.

— 📖 —

The lives of the children I work with have become entangled with mine. Roots grow out of their fingers and hair and entwine around my heart and lungs choking me, making me small again.

I dream that in Julian's behavior plan he gets to earn time with me for not crying. He gets so many points a period for not crying. One day, Julian earns fifteen minutes of time with me. He comes to my office with his aide close behind. He produces the book I have made with him where he can write down private feelings, draw pictures, or scribble.

When I go home at night, I want to be alone. I want to be free of all responsibility. Yet Julian twists his way into my heart and I feel the pressure of pain like water pressing us into flat bodies.

I curl to the side of the bed with the warmth of the hot water bottle against my belly. I breathe in and out with the sound of ocean waves that come through the headphones. I feel like I am an accomplice to a crime. Watching and knowing, but not telling, not shouting out, "This is wrong. This is not the way to heal a child."

Regina and I are having coffee together on a crisp, autumn afternoon. She is taller than I am. We sit across the table from each other. Her face is smooth and browned. I want to reach over and cup her face in my hands. We talk. We laugh. Regina tells me I look tired. She tells me to eat and rest and take care of myself.

The windows of the cafe are misted with rain. Golden leaves and ruby red leaves catch raindrops where they have fallen on the sidewalk outside. I think of our times together as little girls on the couch of my growing-up house, after Sunday school. I don't want to let Regina go.

We finish our coffee and hug. I feel that something lost inside of me has been restored. We part outside, lingering, our fingertips touching.

Jackson — The Back Door to the Heart

If you really want to kill someone, all you gotta do is punch them in the heart. —Jackson, age 5, June 3, 1998.

A T AGE FOUR JACKSON WITNESSED THE ATTEMPTED FIRST-DEGREE murder of his mother. On Valentine's Day, Jackson and his mother, Diane, were sitting in their living room watching T.V. together. Diane's daughter, Ava, seven, was upstairs working on some last minute valentines.

It was dusk when the lights went out. Thinking this was a typical Northwest power outage due to a wind storm, Diane started to get up from the couch to find the candles and matches she kept in the kitchen. She never made it to her feet. As Jackson watched, a shadowy figure entered the living room wearing a ski mask and dark clothing. With both hands the figure brought a butcher knife down on Diane's skull, breaking off the knife handle in the process, and then fled the scene.

Jackson froze as he watched his mother fall into a pool of blood. His sister was still upstairs in her room. The child inched toward the phone on his hands and knees and punched in the numbers 9-1-1 as he had recently been instructed at his preschool class by the medics. (He had often dreamed of becoming a fireman.)

The phone was dead. The intruder had taken care of that.

Jackson ran out the back door. Police found him clawing at the back fence, splinters of wood underneath his fingernails. It was Ava who had run to the neighbors for help after coming downstairs and seeing her mother nearly dead. Jackson, who had witnessed the attack, never got to be the hero.

When Jackson leaves the play therapy room he wants to take some of me with him. He asks, "What can I have?

He pulls a hand-woven basket from Guatemala off the shelf and says, "Can I have this?" He looks down. Ashamed. If I say, "no," for Jackson, it will be like a negation of our time together — a patent rejection. He will think that he is not important enough for me to give him this simple basket. He has told me as much. "You would give it to your own son." It doesn't mean a thing to Jackson when I tell him this is not true. He speaks the language of the heart, not the mind. He wants something of me to carry with him. Anything. In the end, he chooses three paper-clips and leaves happily.

Jackson asks me if I like him, then, "Do you love me?" He risks the question after almost a year of therapy. I tell him that I love him. I am sure that some of my colleagues would tell me I have made a grave clinical mistake. It's not in the rules of therapy to tell clients you love them.

Jackson looks at me with those deer-stuck-in-the-headlights eyes and wants to know why I love him. His eyes are so blue as to be almost transparent. "Why do you love me?" Jackson looks down. Ashamed. How can he be loveable when he didn't save his mother?

"What if I don't have a reason?" I say. "What if I just love you for you?" His five-year-old mind needs a reason. I tell him again: "I love you just because you are Jackson, and there are no other Jacksons like you in the world." This does not satisfy him. He looks up at me. Waiting.

"You have a loving heart, Jackson. You make these incredible worlds in the sandtray. I love it that you come here every week and play and talk with me."

Jackson says, "Do you have anything to eat?"

The first day that Jackson came to therapy he wore a blue, down ski coat with a tear in the sleeve and kept it on during the entire session. It was April and outside the air was still chilly, but inside my office it was warm. I found that traumatized kids often like to keep their coats on even in summer weather. They feel more protected that way.

After I invited Jackson in and showed him the playroom, I asked him if he would draw a picture of himself. He ignored the 8 ½ x 11 inch white paper and crayons I had out on the child's table, and walked up to the large white board hanging on the wall. He stood on a blue plastic chair and took the black marker in his left hand. Jackson began to draw a large rectangle on the board and then drew parallel and horizontal lines delineating an upper and lower story and room in a house.

Next to the sprawl of rectangular house, Jackson drew a neat small house with a pitched roof, doors, symmetrical windows on either side of the door, and smoke coming out of the chimney. This little house seemed like a footnote explaining what an ideal house is really supposed to look like, not the chaotic "house" that was emerging on the board.

Jackson capped the black marker and selected a red one from the tray. He drew two red slashes at intervals along the walls denoting windows and doors. This house appeared to be devoid of anything that conjured up the idea of a home: no flowers, grass, trees, square windows, nor rectangular doors. No smoke from the chimney — classic sign in the drawings of more integrated children.

Next to one red slash, Jackson wrote the numbers 9-1-1.

Jackson started telling me about his drawing in a monotone. He balanced on the chair while I leaned on the wall. His accurate words matched his wiry body. His hair was shaved down close to his skin, and I could see patches of his scalp. The shape of Jackson's skull reminded me of a baby's head formed not too long ago.

Jackson projected the image of a child prematurely toughened by the impact of a traumatic life event. He had a long way to go in therapy. It was difficult for me to find the sweet flavor of innocence in this five-year-old child. His bright, blue eyes often remained in a fixed stare as if Jackson was attempting to transport himself to another world. He had the look of one who is perpetually startled.

As Jackson talked about his house, he became increasingly anxious. He chewed on the collar of his down coat. He talked faster and lost his usual self-consciousness because of his lisp.

Jackson took me through every room of the house explaining its meaning. The red lines marked exits and entrances. Both were problematic for Jackson. He tried to explain: "These red lines are windows. See, I have a lock on my window. It could keep Dan out, but then if he was already in I couldn't get out. The lock is strong and it's hard to move it. I'm not sure I could get out in time."

Jackson looked at me with his blue stare and said, "How old will I be when Dan gets out of prison?"

I wrote a 4 and a 23 next to each other on the white board. Then I added the number 21 to each and added the columns. J=25, D=44. Jackson stood on his chair still staring at the board. This fact did not seem to comfort him. I told him how big I guessed he'd be at twenty-five. "How big?" He wanted to see.

"Well, you're pretty tall at four already; I'd guess you'd be at least as tall and as big as Mr. Simon (the school principal) maybe six-feet two-inches — definitely taller than me."

"But Dan could get out before that. Maybe he could be out now."

It was not unusual for perpetrators of domestic violence to come back for their victims. Diane had told me that Dan had made one last threat before he had nearly taken her life. He would be back to finish her off. She lived in constant fear that he would come back to kill her and her children or send someone from the outside to do the job.

I told Jackson to come down off of the chair. We both sat on the floor. I told Jackson that I knew all about Dan, that his mother had told me the whole story. I didn't know if this was the clinically correct thing to do. I thought it was probably too much for the first session, but I felt Jackson was asking me to bear witness with him to what he had seen.

He had drawn his old house where the assault had taken place. He had not mentally moved into his new house and it would take years for him to do so. I stayed with Jackson all through those years. He still comes to see me now a few times a month.

When I told Jackson that I knew Dan had nearly killed his mother, and that he had watched something no child should ever have to watch, he said, "And the funny thing is she was so covered in blood that I didn't even know it was my mom."

— 📖 —

Jackson no longer acts out the assault of his mother on me. For the first four months of treatment, he would try to scare me or pretend to hurt me or kill me in his play and then make me alive again. This repetitive playing out of the traumatic event is called, "posttraumatic play." After the child gains mastery over the situation and feels empowered, you see a shift in their play and in their emotional life.

Jackson sword fought with me, gunned me down, stabbed me and took a plastic bat again and again to the punching bag I have hanging from my ceiling. He called me a "fucker" and an "asshole" and said, "If you hurt my mom again, I'll kill you."

My job during Jackson's non-directive play therapy was to bear witness. I said things like, "You feel so mad at Dan that you want to kill him."

The turning point in Jackson's play was when he orchestrated a replica of the crime scene in the playroom casting me as his mother and him as Dan. It seemed that for months he had been getting the details just right. On a Tuesday afternoon after six months of treatment, Jackson told me to sit in a chair facing the wall. He took the ponytail holder out of my hair and let it hang loose down my back like his mother's did.

He said, "Stay there," in his most authoritative voice. I played along as the lights went out and I heard the door to my office shut.

Within seconds of shutting the door, it reopened and Jackson burst in. "Don't get up and don't turn around." I followed his directions wondering if he were truly going to knock me out with a vase from the waiting room. Then I felt the edge of his palms pressed together to make a blade coming down straight in the middle of my head. I fell out of my chair onto the floor. Jackson taunted, "Just try to call the police. Just try." I crawled toward my office phone. Jackson said, "Go ahead. Pick it up."

This is not how the real story went. Jackson was trying to correct the situation by having his mother get the help that she needed. I felt tremendous relief. He was healing. He was learning that he wasn't a failure because he hadn't been able to save his mother.

I picked up the receiver and slumped over my desk, held it to my ear. I was startled to find the phone dead. Jackson had re-enacted the scene of the crime so accurately that he had unplugged my phone.

It was an eerie feeling. I could imagine how Jackson must have felt crawling to the phone, dialing 9-1-1 and getting nothing but silence.

I said, "There's no one there, but I'm gonna get the bad guy anyway. I'm gonna get you Dan." At this point I was improvising trying to help Jackson in his effort to get some resolution around a trauma that was impossibly difficult to integrate into his young psyche.

He said, "Ha ha, you can't get me," and pulled a black plastic revolver out of the front of his pants.

I knew that if Jackson used his toy gun on me we'd be back to square one: he'd feel bad that he'd killed me, and he'd remain vigilant and afraid of Dan. I became more directive as the therapist and insisted that Jackson hand the gun over. I was talking him down like you see cops do on T.V. At first he held steady, but I could see the effort it was taking. He kept the gun pointed at me with both hands, tears began to leak from his eyes, but still he stared at me. His arms started to shake a little from the effort of holding them outstretched for so long. It was almost like he was reaching for me instead of trying to kill me.

I spoke softly to Jackson. He had come out of role and was no longer Dan. He was a boy with a gun trained on his mother's head. He let the gun fall and collapsed onto the floor. I approached him slowly and put my hand on the back door to his heart — the place next to the spine where the heart comes through.

The following weeks in therapy, Jackson and I came up with different scenarios where he saved his mother. The phone stayed alive and connected. The lights stayed on, and Jackson became more present each week. He no longer stared so much, but looked me in the eye and showed an array of emotional response from laughing to crying. We both tried to get the bad guy one day and ended tripping over each other and falling into a tangled heap on the floor. In the end Jackson was the hero. He dialed 9-1-1 on my phone for real (while I held the receiver down) and "they"came with toy handcuffs and saved his mom and put Dan in prison forever.

After that session, Jackson started bringing me things. Usually I was offered fries or a sip of his milkshake from Burger King. I got a few Pokemon cards. At Christmas, Jackson watched in delight as I opened a small wooden box to reveal a wooden nutcracker to hang on my tree.

— 📖 —

It's been two years since Jackson has been coming to see me every week. He is a different child. He can look at me and tell me his feelings. He shows incredible empathy for people and symbols of people — dolls.

Last night, Jackson sat me down and prepared us a meal of Playdough soup and pie. He was meticulous in his preparation and gave me ample opportunities to praise his culinary talents. All the dishes were pulled out. He even made me coffee with cream in the miniature tea set, and I took two sugars just so he could have the fun of pretending to scoop it out for me. I thought, this is the same kid that was "kicking my ass" not even six months ago, reverting to terrorizing me with swearing and threatening motions when things were stressing him and triggering memories of the crime scene.

Here we sat, together, Jackson holding a baby whose blue eyes matched his own and opened and shut as he lay her down or brought her to sitting in the crook of his bony boy arm for a bottle.

"How much pie do you want to eat? I'll give you the big piece, but don't forget about the baby, she's gotta eat too." –Jackson, age 7, April 25, 2000

The Tide

I'VE BECOME FEARFUL OF LOSING MYSELF; VENTURING TOO FAR INTO the depths of the children I see in therapy each week, of going too deep into anything. Although I am working part-time outside of the home, (twenty-six hours between two jobs), and the rest of my time is spent mostly with my four-year-old son and six-year-old daughter, I feel the demands placed on me as a mother and a therapist.

I tell myself that I am burned out, but that is one of a thousand concepts written in "therapese." What does it mean? For me it means that I haven't stopped lately.

A normal working day consists of getting my children up and ready for preschool and kindergarten. That means hunting for the one lost shoe, packing lunches, helping with tooth and hair brushing, holding my son on my lap as we watch some T.V., walking my daughter to her bus stop and dropping my son off at his preschool five miles away.

After completing the morning mothering routine, I stop at a drive-through for coffee and head for the elementary school where I work as a counselor. Messages on blue squares of paper are taped to my mailbox. I see that I have six calls on my voice mail. I have a child scheduled for their weekly counseling appointment at 9:30.

Breathe. Stop. Listen. I tell myself, "Allow the tide to roll over you." The tide rises on a platform of pain, years of ageless pain.

While in session, you listen. You receive. You are adult.

After, alone, you start to live what you have heard; what they have lived. Countertransferance. Children shouting or whispering or kicking their secrets to me crescendo into this tide that can roll or crush me depending on the forces of nature at work at the time. The secrets, now particles suspended in the air, surround me like an aura I wear, though I cannot name its color. You're not supposed to. But they tug my own inner pain, my own child. You cannot will it to stop.

I am driving to my second job at a community mental health center. We need the money, but that's not the real reason I am driving to work. I am driving myself closer and closer to my center.

The children I see in therapy have no trouble finding me. They uncover me like I am a Ukrainian stacking doll — the wooden nested dolls that unscrew at the waist in descending sizes until the baby doll is found in the center.

Up ahead is a yellow traffic light. It turns red. I feel the tide beginning to rise inside of me. My fingers clutch the steering wheel — an anchor. My foot eases on the brake. My upper lip is beaded with sweat, the muscles in my forehead tighten as if pulled by a drawstring. Relax, I tell myself. Breathe. Stop. The light is red.

Tina, five years old, came to my office last Tuesday and took the Ukrainian stacking doll apart. She unscrewed the top half of the doll from the bottom. Inside she found the medium-size doll and inside that, the smaller doll with its body and head lacquered in brilliant pinks, blues, and yellows. When Tina opened the smallest doll, she found the only doll in one piece — the baby.

Tina stared at the baby before taking it out and holding it between her thumb and first finger. Then Tina rolled the baby, smooth as a beach rock, between her palms. In this way Tina found me. In this way Tina and I became the same.

The light turns green and the tide recedes into an afternoon shadow. I have a client scheduled at three thirty. I need to get to work. I cannot let the guts of fifteen years of treating children in therapy fall out of me now. But, the sadness tugs at me and the tide threatens once again to flood me.

I am starting to feel that I have done my time, that I have served out the maximum amount of time anyone can stand in "the trenches," — that's another saying in therapese meaning holding the front line, doing battle, doing direct service, meeting face to face with clients and their problems, which smack my psyche sharply into a vivid mirror image that is reflected back to me.

The inside of my car smells of milk gone sour from the coffee with extra cream that dumped into the carpet of my beat up Volvo with 280,000 miles on it. I crank open the window, push the locks down, and flick on the radio. After awhile I give up on trying to find a good station. With the radio off, I fall into the swirl of my own thoughts.

I picture my daughter in her new school shoes, black hush puppies with a T-strap that she still needs help buckling every morning. My son at preschool, pale, coughing, avoiding the rougher boys. I feel his forehead in my mind, and it is hot. I think of my husband riding his bike, his legs pumping blood and oxygen all through his body. I think of the elementary school that I just left, but not before I made sure that Alex got breakfast in the nurse's office, and I had returned the pile of phone messages on my desk. My head swims with the names and faces of children, my own and all the others, each one, this child of mine.

I have agreed to help out with an overload of intake appointments at the community mental health center. I have trouble finding parking on the congested urban streets that surround the clinic. Halfway houses for the chronically mentally ill abound and I slam my brakes on for a man shuffling across the street sucking a cigarette down to the filter.

The tide rises again flooding me with memories of my oldest brother who has never made it to a halfway house, but alternates his time as a resident of inpatient lock-up units or time on an estate where he does odd jobs.

This man crossing in front of my car looks about the same age as my brother, forty-four. The erosion of the body and the mind that goes with schizophrenia makes my brother and this man look much older than they really are.

I never have found my brother's center. There has been too much turbulence around him to get close. It is because of him that I have chosen the profession I am in or, more likely, it chose me. I thought I could heal my brother with love and that would be enough. I didn't understand why he didn't get better. I thought that maybe I started too late with him, so when I went back to school to become a mental health counselor I decided that I wanted to work with younger children.

I found that even a child of two or three can be hard to find — their essence already buried under layers of trauma and distrust. Still, it is easier for me to access the younger children as I am myself a child easily uncovered like the doll that screws apart in the middle. If I become the child, if I become the body of the thing that contains all that is human and real, then I become the healer and there is magic.

I park with the tail end of my car sticking out along the curb. I don't care if I get a ticket. I don't want to be late for my first meeting with a new client. I tell myself to breathe. I tell the tide to stop rising. I tell myself to become the water, to equalize the tide.

I step out into the street and into a bolt of strong sunshine that warms me to my core. I close my eyes and take a deep breath and feel the sun on my face. When I open my eyes I am looking at the balcony of the clinic where several staff are having a cigarette break.

I look at my watch and see that it is 3:28. I reach into the car and haul out my briefcase uncovering one of my son's plastic action heroes. I smile. The cement is dry and firm under my feet. The tide recedes as I walk toward Building A to get the file on my 3:30.

Billie

MANY OF MY PSYCHOLOGICAL ASSESSMENTS AT THE Community Mental Health Center are for kids with "ODD." ODD is short for Oppositional Defiant Disorder. Number 313.81 for the insurance company's billings. Page 91 in The Diagnostic and Statistical Manual of Mental Disorders, (fourth edition), otherwise known as the DSM-IV. I have the page number memorized. This is what it says:

> A. A pattern of negativistic, hostile, and defiant behavior lasting at least six months, during which four (or more) of the following are present: 1. often loses temper, 2. often argues with adults, 3. often actively defies or refuses to comply with adults' requests or rules, 4. often deliberately annoys people, 5. often blames others for his or her mistakes or misbehavior, 6. is often touchy or easily annoyed by others, 7. is often angry and resentful, 8. is often spiteful or vindictive.....

The telephone screener on my three-thirty appointment had said, "Quite ODD." I wondered how old the kid was. I wondered how big the kid was. However, the criteria for ODD sounded, in many ways, like the profile of an average teenage kid. In my intakes with ODD kids, that is what I usually found — a troubled teenager with a background ranging from unfortunate to horrific. I pull Billie Hammond's telephone screen sheet out of my briefcase: "Thirteen-year-old black male. Foster mother is requesting help in managing client's out-of-control behavior. Client has been prescribed meds but is non-compliant with taking them. Client is expelled from school for assaulting principal. Client has a history of acting-out, non-compliance, disrespectful to authorities, and truancy. Client has recently been in juvie [Juvenile Court] for bringing a weapon to school. Diagnosis: ODD. Rule out Conduct Disorder."

Conduct Disorder is reserved for the kids with out-of-control behavior extreme enough to be a danger to self or others (i.e. destroying property, aggressive to "people and animals," fire setting, etc). Billie was not listed as Conduct Disordered. I'd had lots of kids with ODD that looked real bad on paper, but were scared and disturbed teenagers when I met them face-to-face.

I put down my briefcase and set my coffee-to-go on top of the filing cabinet. Pulling out Billie's file is like unearthing a boulder. "The File," is actually three files rubber-banded together to make an eight-to-ten inch mountain of paper.

I sling my briefcase over one shoulder and hug the compact version of Billie Hammond to my chest. I unlock the door to Treatment Room 314 and thunk the two pound document onto the desk. I sit down in a threadbare upholstered chair with nicks in the wooden arms. I look down at the brown carpet and around the room at the bare off-white walls. I wonder what it feels like to be a child entering this room. A small basket of toys sits in one corner of the office; a cheap plastic doll with a hole in her mouth for a bottle, some Hot Wheels, and some crayons and markers.

I turn my back on the room and focus on the files in front of me on the desk. I start to undo the rubber band and then decide that it might be best if I don't have any preconceived notion of Billie Hammond. Obviously he has been in treatment for a long time to have a record of this length. Why not start fresh. Give the kid a new start.

As I wait for the receptionist to call me and notify me of my client's arrival, my curiosity takes over and I pull back a corner of the first file and read clips of sentences. Of course, nothing makes sense this way so I fold the corner back and let my hands rest on top of the stiff cardboard cover of Billie's life.

As I sit and wait for Billie to arrive, the image of a toddler I once cared for in a treatment center for abused and neglected children keeps coming into my mind. It has been ten years since

I worked at that treatment center and I sometimes wonder how the kids who had been there are doing now.

I remember the slap of bare feet on cold gray tile. I remember the laughter and the tears coming from a roomful of two and three year olds. I remember the smells of macaroni and cheese and canned green beans, soiled diapers, and Lysol. I remember the little boy, Billie Hammond.

I am sure of it now. I was Billie's social worker when he was two years old. In my mind, the image is crystal clear: a bare-chested, dark-skinned boy in a disposable diaper, barefoot and disoriented from his nap, standing near the changing table on chubby toddler legs. Billie; a permanent down turning of his pale lips. Alternately an angry intensity and an emptiness in his muddy brown eyes. Nubby knots of hair on his head. Didn't want to be held. Difficult to console after a tantrum. The boy who dumped his lunch of spaghetti on his head and ground the noodles and sauce into his bristly hair and smeared the goop on his chest and then refused a bath.

Billie never knew his father. His mother was a prostitute and a drug addict. At two years old, Billie had lived in three different foster homes and was a ward of the State. Parental rights had been terminated.

— 📖 —

At 3:44, I go out to the waiting area to see if Billie and his foster mother, Mrs. Adams, have arrived. They haven't. I return to room 314 and try to focus on some paperwork, but I keep seeing Billie by the changing table rubbing sleep out of his eyes. It seems as though the tide has disappeared. It is only gathering. At 3:50 my phone rings. It is the receptionist announcing Billie's arrival.

All of the chairs in the waiting area are filled with the lanky bodies of adolescent boys. I look around and find a woman seated to my right.

"Hi. You must be Mrs. Adams. I'm Martha Wakenshaw. Which one is Billie?" I thought I would have recognized him right away.

"This one here is Billie." Mrs. Adams says, pointing to a handsome young boy of thirteen who has his arms wrapped around a basketball.

"Hi Billie. I'm Martha. I'll be doing your assessment." I smile broadly. The basketball drops from Billie's grasp, and he crosses his arms over his chest and scowls at me.

"Come on," Mrs. Adams coaxes. "You need to go with this lady."

Billie looks up at me and it is the same Billie I knew as a toddler. He has grown a pencil thin mustache on his upper lip and his hair has been shaved close to the scalp in a cap of black smoothness. His body is all muscle in gym shorts and a T-shirt.

Billie slumps in his chair and refuses to move.

I wait.

Billie remains in his seat with his arms crossed over his chest.

The mats have been set down for nap time. Billie's mat is pushed against the back of the bookshelf. He is one of the most volatile children in the toddler room and often throws a tantrum at nap time. Today Billie lies down on his mat on his side and his face looks gray with the lights turned out and the shades pulled part of the way down. Today Billie goes down easy. I sit on the edge of his mat and rub his back. It is summer and his skin feels warm and smooth. Billie falls asleep with my hand resting on the small of his back. The heat that comes through my palm feels good. I don't want to take my hand away.

"Let's go down to the gym and shoot some hoop," Billie says.

"We really need to get this done, first," I say, indicating the green file.

Billie rolls his eyes.

"The sooner you get this done," Mrs. Adams said, "the sooner you can go home and play all the basketball you want to."

Billie sits up a little in his chair. He gets to his feet and drags himself into room 314 and plunks himself into the chair nearest mine. Mrs. Adams sits nearest to the door. The treatment room is about as big as a small walk-in closet. All of our knees are nearly touching.

I immediately wish for more room. The space feels claustrophobic. Billie is slouched down in his chair again. I dread barraging him with questions that he has probably heard a hundred times before.

"I know you've had to answer these questions before," I say, pointing to the mountain of paper at my elbow on the desk. "But, in order to readmit you, we need to go through this one more time and see if anything has changed."

"Ain't nothin' changed," Billie barks.

"Okay. Let's start with who's in the home right now. Who do you live with, Billie, besides, Mrs. Adams?"

"She fuckin' ate Kung Pao Chicken and made us eat Ramen. She's mean. Am I right? You eatin' yo' Kung Pao Chicken and fuck man—"

"Watch yo' mouth, man," Mrs. Adams says in a controlled monotone.

"So, you live with Mrs. Adams and—"

Billie interrupts me. "Janelle. She's Janelle. What's with this fuckin' 'Mrs. Adams' shit?"

"So, you live with Janelle and... How old are you Billie? Why don't we start with that?"

"Twelve."

As soon as I finish writing twelve, Billie says, "Thirteen." I scratch out twelve and write, thirteen. "No, I'm twelve," Billie says.

I put down my pen and say, "You know Billie this really isn't going too well."

Janelle turns to Billie and says, "You quit jivin' with her boy. This woman's here to help you with your problems. You hear?"

"I don't got no problems. You got all the problems. You was the one who ate yo' Kung Pao Chicken and gave us Ramen. Man..."

Billie leans in towards me. "Why can't we shoot hoop? Man... We could be doin this shit in the gym."

The room is feeling smaller and I open the door for some air.

"I don't have to live with you ya know. Hey! Nellie," Billie raises his voice. I said, "I don't have to take this shit no mo'."

Janelle remains unruffled, her voice strong, her face smooth and unlined. "Yeah. Go on then. Run. I'll still love you anyway, and I'll still come and visit you."

Billie shifts around in his seat and starts arguing loudly with his foster mother. "I can run you know. Fuck DSHS. Fuck them. Eatin' Kung Pao Chicken. I still can't believe it." Then Billie focuses his attention on me, "So, come on. Let's go play ball."

My breath is starting to come in short shallow gulps. My heart is racing with the sheer power of this boy's anger. I keep looking into his face and seeing baby Billie. Now all the puffiness of his face is gone. His cheekbones stand out sharply and the chubby legs of toddlerhood are streamlined into sinuous muscle.

"I know you Billie. I know you from a long time ago." I wait for some recognition.

Billie stops his jive for a moment and looks at me, his angry glare temporarily suspended.

"What is this shit?" Billie asks.

Janelle looks straight ahead and says, "Watch yo' mouth boy. Can't you see this woman is just tryin' to do her job?"

"Did you go to Kid's Place? You know when you were really really little. You went to Kid's Place and I was your teacher. I remember you Billie."

"I never did go to that shit-ass school. What the hell is you talkin' about?"

Janelle: "I'm tellin you, man, watch yo' mouth."

"I ain't never gone there, that's all I'm sayin', Nellie."

"Yes, you did too go there. You don't know what you're talkin' about. You were just a baby. You sure did go to that school. This lady here ain't stupid. Okay?"

"So anyway, Billie. I remember you and it's good to see you again."

Billie broods awhile and looks at the floor. "This is bullshit," he says, "total one hundred percent fucked up bullshit."

I feel cornered. Billie leans in. His elbows press on his knees. I'm feeling the tide begin to rise. We have only gotten as far as name, age, refuses meds, foster mother requests a psych. eval. (again). I try one more time: "Why are you here, Billie?"

"Because she thinks I'm all fucked up," Billie says pointing to Janelle.

"Why do *you* think you're here?" I persist.

Billie turns to Janelle then back to me then back to Janelle, his fists clenched.

I stand up aware of the tightness in my jaw.

"Less go," Billie says to Janelle. "You just tryin' to impress these white folks."

I stand smoothing my pants with my hands. I stall for a little more time, hoping that Billie will miraculously decide he does in fact want to cooperate with me. No chance.

"Excuse me, " I say to Janelle. "I'll be right back."

Janelle grabs me by the arm. "Wait a minute, please," she says. "Let me see your back."

Janelle pats her fingers all across my back and down the legs of my pants and gently touches the small of my back. She rakes her fingers through my long hair and then, glaring at Billie, says, "You gooked her. You gooked her. Here this lady is trying to do a decent job and you gooked her."

I feel helpless and dumb. I don't know what the word, "gooked," means. Then I feel the wetness on my cheek and reach around to touch Billie's spit globs on my back and in my hair and dripping down the legs of my pants. I bolt out of the room and break into sobs. I pass clients and therapists in the hall and try to explain, but no words will come. The tide has broken stronger than ever, and I am drowning.

I see a supervisor on her way to the coffeepot and say, "Linda, I need you now." I am crying like a baby. All the pain of the years of doing child welfare work "in the trenches," and "on the front line," come flooding through me. I see Billie in diapers. Then, as if a time-lapse camera had presented the boy ten years later, in the space of a millisecond, I see Billie now.

Cry

ILLIE RUNS THROUGH THE AGENCY PULLING OTHER CHILDREN'S drawings off the walls and butting staff he passes in the hallway. He is out the door and wandering around the small campus when the crisis team catches up with him and are able to contain him.

The crisis team has their offices downstairs and I am glad for their presence. It feels like every kid that comes through the agency's doors is in crisis, but the team's energy is reserved for the "real crisis" — officially, when a child is "a danger to himself or others."

I find an empty office and sit down, holding my pounding head in my hands. Tears drip onto my pants. I feel something release like a lever has been pulled back in the part of my brain that holds the memories of bruised and beaten children, children traded for sex in return for crack, children starved and left alone for days in soiled diapers that cut deep sores into their bottoms. It just keeps re-generating. I feel like all of my efforts have been useless.

I cry, and when I get done crying, I emerge to pick up the pieces of Billie's assessment.

As I walk out into the waiting area, I see Joe, a boy of about eleven, cutting paper into tiny and tinier pieces until the carpet is littered with white confetti. I wonder who has given him scissors. The receptionist is talking on the phone. She holds her palm over the receiver for a moment and tells me that a supervisor is finishing Billie's assessment.

Several families are waiting to be seen by their therapists.

Parents and foster parents, grandparents, and children of all ages sit in chairs that line the walls. Because Joe has taken over all of the floor space and is wielding a pair of sharp scissors, the other children stay close to their caretakers and do not play with toys on the floor.

My eyes are swollen with crying. My face is blotchy and red, and I shake my hair out from my ponytail to try and hide my grief. I need to be strong. I have a job to do: de-escalating Joe, who is one of Billie's younger foster brothers.

I crouch down on the floor next to Joe and say, "Hi." I look up and watch the clients who are watching me as they wait for their therapists. "Hi," I say again and this time Joe answers with a barely audible, "Hi."

Joe has white, freckled skin and carmel-colored hair. His right eye wanders when he looks at me.

"Joe" I say, "I'm Martha. Here's the deal. If I help you pick up all of this paper, we can draw together, how's that?"

Joe smiles and makes some guttural noises. "Okay."

I get down on the floor and start picking up. To my surprise, Joe starts picking up, too. He becomes absorbed in his task and picks up even the tiniest slivers of paper that I would have left for the janitor to vacuum up later. Joe is so lost in his work that he lays down the scissors, and I quickly swoop them up and on to the receptionist's desk.

I am thinking that I will not get paid for today's work, because when you work contract you only get paid when you complete an assessment.

A member of the crisis team that knows Joe stoops down and whispers to me, "Not to worry; Joe is so delayed, he's harmless. He has an I.Q. of about seventy — definitely delayed."

Joe's voice startles me, but more than that what he says to me is amazing. As if he has heard what the other counselor said, Joe says to me in his deep voice, "You know how you should have handled Billie? Oh, I know Billie. He's a manipulator, he's a liar, and he's a natural born killer. He spit on you, ha ha," and Joe bursts into a big grin. He goes on, "I'm tellin you — this is how you handle Billie..." Joe speaks robotically with measured syllables as if a metronome is tapping out the slow rhythm of his speech. He speaks carefully and without inflection. His eyes dance every now and then when he is making a particularly important point.

"Here's how you handle Billie. Ah, he spit on you. He spit on you. Okay you pick up the phone and you call CPS. That's what works with Billie."

I consider Joe's words and say, "You know Joe, you are one smart cookie. Let's go draw."

The waiting area is spotless. I grab some markers and a few sheets of paper out of the recycling box by the Xerox machine. Joe follows me into the vacant supervisor's office, and we sit on the floor drawing pictures together. A crisis team member perusing the area gives me a "thumbs up," and I begin to relax.

Joe wants me to write a letter for him to his former therapist who has left the agency. I say, "Why don't you write it yourself?" and he looks down and says, "Just you write it. I'll tell you what to say." I pick up a purple marker and wait for Joe's instruction.

"Write: Dear Karen. I miss you. I love you. When will you come back? I live at Mrs. Adams' house. You know, it's blue. I love you. Please visit me. You remember I am Joe. Love, Joe."

I write down the words and Joe beams. He takes the marker from me and scrawls, "J-O-E," in big block letters. I feel the same way as when I play on the floor with my three-year-old son. There is a sweet innocence about Joe.

Next, Joe wants me to draw the stems of flowers and then let him fill in the petals. We work like this for about twenty minutes, and then I know Joe is getting restless because he asks for scissors to cut up more paper. "Let's go for a walk instead," I suggest and Joe willingly agrees.

We walk down to the large open room where all the contract workers have mailboxes. I tell Joe to wait outside the door, while I put the letter for Karen in her mailbox. I tell Joe that even though she is gone, she still comes in to pick up her mail.

As we are walking down the hall, Billie comes racing around a corner. He reaches my face on tiptoe, grabs my arm and says,

"I'm sorry." I feel Joe flinch and move closer to me. In a second, Billie has Joe in a head lock and pounds him against the door of the bathroom. He spits in Joe's face and yells, "You fuckin' little bastard, I should just kill you right now."

Joe is like a limp rag in Billie's hands. I try to pry Billie off of Joe, but he spits into my eye and continues banging Joe's head into the door. The crisis "team'" comes down the hall: a woman, slight with blond hair. She shouts, "Billie, get the hell out of this building before you do anymore damage."

Billie races down the stairs. Joe is left trembling and whimpering by my side.

Mrs. Adams comes to collect Joe and shakes her head when she hears what Billie has done. "I love that boy, but he got to learn. This just ain't right." She puts her arm around Joe and as they descend the stairway to leave, Joe shouts to me, "Write Heims on the picture (he has given me a picture of some flowers signed J-O-E). I think it begins with an "H." Then he adds in his measured tone, "I think you'd make a very good couns-lor and you should get a lot of bizness."

— 📖 —

As I walk to my car I see a white paper under the windshield wiper. Damn. They gave me a parking ticket. I rip the ticket off the windshield and throw it with my briefcase on the passenger's seat. When I'm halfway home, I look at the ticket: $22.00.

I avoid the freeway and take the long way home. I need some time to clear my head. I can still feel Billie's spit on me. I wipe at my eye with the sleeve of my sweater. I don't want to go home to my own kids like this, all covered in spit, my brain churning up every cuss word there ever was told to me by a thirteen-year-old boy I knew as a toddler.

My husband is tired of hearing tales from the war zone. I think about how nuts it is that I am doing this work. Billie reminds me of how long I have been working on the front lines. So many years have passed. I've worked with hundreds of abused and neglected kids, and I still collapse in pain over the injustice of it all. I can't solve "it." I can't cure them. I cannot answer all the "why's."

My hair feels sticky from Billie's spit, and I have an urge to wash; wash my hair, wash my clothes, wash my body. The urge becomes an obsession. I want to tear my sweater off in the car.

I pull abruptly into a salon parking lot and the driver in the car behind me honks and gives me the finger.

The sign says, "Tanning, Haircuts, Perms." I go in and sign up for a wash and a cut. An elderly woman takes her time writing my name down in the appointment book and makes sure to get the spelling right. I feel so cared for in that small act.

I sit down in a plastic chair to wait my turn. I leaf through a *People's Magazine* and think of Billie. I ask for the restroom and wash my face and hands and blot my sweater with a paper towel.

When the beautician calls me she takes time to ask me if I want coffee and what would I like in it and what do I want done with my hair. Memories of today and the days before this come flooding back. I don't want to think of all the maltreated kids I have worked with. I just want to think about my hair.

A Thousand Paper Cranes

WHEN I GET HOME IT IS RAINING THE SOFT NORTHWEST RAIN that comes down like a fairy mist coating the ferns and pines and releasing their scent into the night air. The windows in our restored farmhouse glow. It is spring, and the earth is fragrant with the musty and pungent odors of birth.

I stand in the back garden until I am soaked through with rain. I take my shoes and socks off and dig my toes into the earth. This must be what it feels like for a child to sink their hands into Playdough — a gentle anchoring connection to some elemental remembrance.

My belly is soft, my shoulders relaxed, they have given up the fight. Standing with my feet rooted to the earth in the middle of the garden that my husband has planted, I catch the scent of lavender, pick a sprig and twine it into my dripping hair. I reach out and touch the prickly blue grasses he has planted and let the thorn of a rose prick my finger and taste its blood. It's been a long time since I have allowed myself to feel.

My pants stick to my legs. I unbutton the sweater that I was wearing when Billie spit on me. I drape it over a rock and decide to leave it there overnight.

From the reflection of the kitchen lights I can see the chalk drawings that my children have made earlier on our cement steps. Pink and green pastels run together with blue into a puddle that was once a rainbow. Even when my son draws a scary monster at school he places a rainbow in its left hand. My daughter likes to write her name with chalk on cement or with a stick in the sand at the beach or on my back with her fingers when I am tucking her in at night. Everywhere she goes she finds a way to write her name.

I've left my watch in the car. The last thing I want to feel is time. I have been driven by time and schedules and that is why the tide has overtaken me. I can't do the work I do and not stop to reflect and feel. It's a paradox; the feelings I have as a therapist. In session, the feelings come quick and sharp and acutely painful, but must be eclipsed if I am to do the work I need to with the child. But they go deep, deep inside me and get buried there. Feelings, like the kids I work with, can only be let out when it is safe. It is my job to create a safe place for children. I cannot do that when my own guts are spilling out. Today, I see how critical it is to create safety for myself if I am to continue.

My face feels that good kind of prickly cold and I lift it to the black sky, my eyes closed, rain washing my eyelids and running down my cheeks. Raising my arms overhead I arch back, placing my palms on my sacrum and then foreward into a swan dive. My yoga. The rain is warm and lubricates my joints. I thrust my right leg back into a lunge and then, exhaling deeply, push myself up into the tent-like position of downward-facing dog. My breath is audible like the whisper of the ocean and, continuing with this breath flow, I ease into plank pose, then down on my belly and into cobra. My heart touches the cold earth and is jolted awake. Resting there for a moment, I feel the sensation of aliveness. This is what plants must feel: the contact with the earth. I realize I have lost this. Inside my heart has become sluggish and muddy. The closeness with the earth renews my strength. Again, my face turns upward and rain splashes on my forehead. Exhaling back into dog, I flow into a foreward bend, my nose touching my knees, my hands planted on the ground. Rolling my spine, my head is the last to come up and rests like a flower on its stem. My hands come together at my heart in *namaste* — the sign of self-blessing. I have just completed *Surya Namaskar*: sun salutation. It is time to go inside.

Inside, the house is warm and I can feel the presence of my family although all I can see is a clutter of the aftermath of dinnertime on the kitchen table. I recognize my children's plates right away, small mounds of mashed potatoes pushed around with peas imbedded. Gnawed pieces of chicken, some chewed and spit back out, and crumbs of biscuits with drippings of butter and honey that have been eaten first and filled their bellies.

Napkins lay crumpled on the oak tabletop stained with tempera paint. A soaked purple dishrag tells me that Charlie's juice has spilled again. My husband's plate is clean and stacked neatly by the sink.

I automatically start to clear the dishes and then stop. I put down a plate that I am holding and seat myself at the table enjoying the mess of my loved ones. There is something comforting about the disorder that follows a meal.

A basket of biscuits remains wrapped in a white cotton cloth on the table. I place my hand on the cloth and bury my face in the basket. I dry the rain and tears from my eyes. I am reminded of my daughter's baby blanket, the sweet, yeasty smell that babies carry like little balls of dough. My hands are dirty from resting in the wet earth and the mingling aromas of all that is essential floods my heart with fiery warmth.

I have lost all track of time. I hear the low tones of my husband's voice reading to the children. It must be bedtime. His voice comes down the hallway and into the warm kitchen in a humming vibration. I can't really hear his words until he says, "Goodnight, I love you," and I picture him tucking Molly Rose and Charlie in and kissing their foreheads, my son saying, "Big hug, Daddy." My daughter, "Can you make me peanut and butter and jelly for lunch tomorrow?"

"God is in the details" was meant differently. I understand it better.

Starting to feel the chill from the rain, I peel off my clothes. My children are sleeping. My husband draws a bath for me. He leads me to the tub wrapped in a towel and I sink in the steamy water up to my chin.

As a child therapist, I need to learn the way of the heart. My heart gets seared when it is too open. I shut down when my heart gets too saturated with the pain of the young children I see as I breathe in their stories and forget to exhale them out. They get so close that they can touch me. They can take their finger and brush away that fine layer of dust that protects the heart.

Their small hands reach for me and I take them, their offering, and fold them into me. It is a natural maternal response. But I can't work this way for long — giving so much of myself. I am too open. My heart gets broken fifty times a day.

I get out of my bath and, wrapping myself in a thick terry robe, check on my children. Molly Rose is sleeping in her new sweatshirt that she wears twenty-four hours a day. Her breathing is so quiet as to be barely audible. I press my ear to her chest to listen. Charlie has flung his covers off and is hugging the rainbow dinosaur that he got from his dad when he was born. He has taken to wrapping the dinosaur in his thread-bare receiving blanket, just as we once wrapped him.

My stepson, Patrick, is sixteen. He knows everything there is to know about movies and the history of cinematography. When I emerge from my bath he is sitting at the kitchen table with scraps of blue, purple, yellow, and pink rice paper. He has always been good with his hands and tonight he is working on many intricate folds. There seems to be some sort of head to this paper creature and then he holds up the angled shape and pulls firmly down on the wings to reveal a paper origami crane.

"A kid at school has cancer and we're making a thousand paper cranes for good luck. There's this Japanese tradition that started when this girl, Sadako, died from the atom bomb disease — you know, leukemia — when she was twelve. If we fold a thousand paper cranes, Brian will get well."

A Ritual to Read to Each Other

If you don't know the kind of person I am
and I don't know the kind of person you are
a pattern that others made may prevail in the world
and following the wrong god home we may miss our star.

For there is many a small betrayal in the mind
a shrug that lets the fragile sequence break
sending with shouts the horrible errors of childhood
storming out to play through the broken dike.

And as elephant parade holding each elephant's tail
but if one wanders through the circus won't find the park,
I call it cruel and maybe the root of all cruelty
to know what occurs but not recognize the fact.

And so I appeal to a voice, to something shadowy
a remote important region in all who talk:
though we could fool each other, we should consider —
lest the parade of our mutual life get lost in the dark.

For it is important that awake people be awake,
or a breaking line may discourage them back to sleep,
the signals we give — yes, no, or maybe —
should be clear; the darkness around us is deep.

–William Stafford

Appendix

PROGRAMS THAT MAKE A DIFFERENCE:

NATIONAL COMMITTEE
FOR THE PREVENTION OF CHILD ABUSE
Anne Cohn-Donnelly
322 S. Michigan, Suite 1600
Chicago, IL 60604
(312) 663-3520

THE CHILDREN'S HEALTH FUND
Irwin Redliner, President
317 E. 64th Street
New York, NY 10021
(212) 535-9400
FAX (212) 535-7488

HEALTHY START
Gladys Wong, Director
2881 Waimano Home Road
Pearl City, HI 96782
(808) 453-6020

ZERO TO THREE
Matthew Melmud, Director
734 15th Street, Suite 1000
Washington, DC 20005
(202) 638-1144

THE FATHERHOOD PROJECT
Families and Work Institute
307 7th Avenue, Suite 1906
New York, NY 10001
(212) 465-2044
www.fatherhoodproject.org/

ANNIE B. CASEY FOUNDATION
701 Paul Street
Baltimore, MD 21201
(410) 223-2890

DATA AND STATISTICS
ON CHILD WELFARE IN AMERICA:

KIDS COUNT DATA BOOK
The Annie B. Casey Foundation
701 Paul Street
Baltimore, MD 21201
(410) 223-2890

THE FUTURE OF CHILDREN
The David and Lucille Packard Foundation
300 Second Street, Suite 102
Los Altos, CA 94022
(415) 948-3696

THE STATE OF AMERICA'S CHILDREN YEARBOOK
The Children's Defense Fund
25 E. Street N.W.
Washington, D.C. 20001
(202) 628-8787

About the Author

Martha Wakenshaw is a psychotherapist in private practice in Shoreline, Washington, specializing in play and expressive arts therapy. A graduate of Seattle University in counseling psychology (MA 1988) and psychology (BA 1979), Connecticut College, Wakenshaw is a board-certified mental health counselor with fifteen years of experience as a child mental health professional.

The author's previous work includes a monthly column ("Mental Health Matters") for Seattle's *The Voice,* numerous articles on child care and community needs, and experience gained as a research assistant for Dr. Eliana Gil's book *Moving Mountains — Using Expressive Arts Therapies with Abused Children.* She is also an award-winning poet.

Prior to starting her own practice, Wakenshaw worked as a case manager and program director of a therapeutic childcare center serving abused and neglected preschoolers. Additionally, the author was employed by a major school district as family advocate. Her experience as a residential treatment therapist working with adolescents provided the foundation for her career working with emotionally disturbed children and those in trauma due to family violence, abuse, or other social factors.

Wakenshaw and her husband live with their three children in the Seattle area.

From the Publisher

If you've enjoyed reading *This Child of Mine: A Therapist's Journey* by Martha Wakenshaw, then consider purchasing another fine book from Harbinger Press, such as *Where's Daddy? The Mythologies behind Custody-Access-Support* by K.C.

"*Where's Daddy?* cuts right to the heart of one of the most pivotal and controversial issues in today's society. Children unquestionably need the influence of both parents in their lives to be balanced. Hopefully, *Where's Daddy?* will finally open eyes to many of the unfair biases that exist in our legal systems today. As a divorced father, having dealt with these issues personally, I applaud K.C.'s insightful treatment of this life-shaping issue."

–Richard McCall, Ph.D. psychologist, Zen Master, *Shihan*, President, Zen-Mind International, Inc., author, *Secrets of Samurai Parenting*, father

Where's Daddy?
The Mythologies behind Custody-Access-Support

K.C.

ISBN: 0-9674736-5-9 Cloth, 256 pages
$26.50 US ($34.95 Can)

Additional Copies

Phone:	800-247-6553 / 419-281-1802
Web:	http://www.harbpress.com
E-mail:	order@bookmaster.com
Fax:	419-281-6883
Mail:	BookMasters, Inc.
	P.O. Box 388
	Ashland, OH 44805 USA

For e-mail, fax or mail, fill in and submit the following.
Cheques may be in US or Canadian dollars, payable to BookMasters Inc.

This Child of Mine   ISBN 0-9674736-0-8
US: $12.95   Can: $19.95
Plus shipping and handling; amount varies with destination.*
Virginia and Ohio residents, add state sales tax.

Number of Copies:_____

Name:_____

Address:_____

City:_____ State /Province:_____

Zip / Postal Code:_____ Country:_____

Charge Card: _VISA   _MastrCard   _AmerExpr   _Discover

Card Number:_____ Exp:_____
mm/yy

Name on card if different from above:_____

Signature:_____

* S&H for up to 3 copies: within US, $3.95 US$; to Canada, $7.95 Can$;
overseas, $8.00 US$.